The Neighborhood Church

The Neighborhood Church

God's Vision of Success

ROBERT G. MOSS

FOREWORD BY
CRAIG VAN GELDER

WIPF & STOCK · Eugene, Oregon

THE NEIGHBORHOOD CHURCH
God's Vision of Success

Wipf and Stock
An Imprint of Wipf and Stock Publishers
199 W. 8th Ave., Suite 3
Eugene, OR 97401

www.wipfandstock.com

ISBN 13: 978-1-62564-945-4

Manufactured in the U.S.A.   09/04/2014

To Lutheran Church of the Master, Lakewood, Colorado, for
your support, patience, grace, willingness to try anything,
and especially your forgiveness throughout this project

Contents

Foreword

THE CONVERSATION ABOUT THE church today continues to be obsessed with how to fix congregations to make them somehow *right* for engaging in mission in their local contexts in order to be successful. There are an abundance of books being published along these lines, with recent examples including: *Deep Church, Simple Church, Externally-Focused Church, Deliberate Church, Hybrid Church, Church 3.0, Organic Church, Total Church,* and the list goes on. The basic instinct giving birth to this literature has some merit—congregations need to be deeply engaged with their local contexts. But the theologically-framing of the argument being made is typically quite anemic—focusing primarily on either a Christology that promotes the great commission or, if Trinitarian in understanding, tends to default to a sending God. In addition, the focus of attention is typically misdirected in trying to *fix* the church *before* attempting to engage the context.

This present volume stands in stark contrast to this understanding and these approaches. The author draws deeply from a robust Trinitarian understanding of the social reality of God to invite a relational approach to ministry by congregations within their contexts—a *perichoretic* relationship. This is a relational approach that involves mutuality and which invites shared learning. Rather than starting with the local congregation to address the issues, the author starts with the local context—the neighborhood or neighborhoods in which a congregation is located. We are invited to think biblically and theologically in very practical ways about the God questions: What is God doing? and What is God trying to do? These questions fundamentally change the conversation by placing the focus on a congregation engaging in Spirit-led discernment in order to discover, understand, and learn about and from its local context—thus learning to develop a reciprocal relationship with the neighbors in its context. The argument is that God is already out ahead of us within this context and a congregation's role is to discern and discover what this is all about.

This approach turns the discussion about success on its head and replaces it with a much more substantive understanding of ministry—partnering with the Holy Spirit to participate more fully in God's mission in the world. But the author doesn't just offer this perspective as a helpful framework. He proceeds to provide multiple practical tools for engaging in this process in what he refers to as "learning to listen" by: taking a walk, hosting a town hall meeting, engaging in interviews, riding along with police, and hanging out at the local stylist shop. All of these practice steps are consistently developed as actions to be taken by a team of persons who are learning together how to discern the Spirit's work and presence within their local context. These steps are also consistently developed within the methodology of action learning—having the group reflect carefully on what it is learning as it continues to design new ways to listen to and learn from its neighbors even while sharing what is being learned with the larger congregation.

This is a very substantive theologically-informative practical guide for congregations who want to move past the endless search for solutions that promise success, but which seldom do. It is a guide for congregations to engage deeply in relationship with the Triune God as they learn to engage deeply with their neighbors in their local context. I heartily commend this book to those leaders of congregations who want to take seriously the mission of the Triune God within any and every local context and who are looking for hands-on practices for being able to engage in this work.

Craig Van Gelder, PhD

Preface

THIS IS A BOOK about congregational change. Specifically, change about our understanding of our purpose as the church. It may be presumptuous to start it by saying that this has been needed for seventeen hundred years. Be that as it may, that's where I'm starting. Without a doubt, there are things the church has done well over the centuries in accordance with the reign of God: developing education, advancing health care, feeding the hungry and clothing the naked, enhancing disaster relief, and standing with the poor are chief among these. In so doing we've proclaimed the gospel of Jesus Christ with clarity and love. Yes, sometimes God's mercy and compassion are made real in the lives of people all over this planet through the work of Christ's church.

And yet with a history of all this for twenty centuries, the Christian church continues to decline in numbers. Are we doing something wrong? Do we need to work harder? Do we need to do something different? Do we need to do something better? Should we be worried?

The decline in numbers of American Christianity has little to do with inefficiency or laziness. Churches and church leaders are working harder and longer than ever before—to the point of rostered leaders burning out at an alarming rate. That, however, is a topic for another book. Our numerical decline has nothing to do with our faith or faith practices. And it's not because we aren't teaching our children well enough, aren't relevant enough, don't have updated projection or sound systems in our worship areas, or don't have enough programs for young adults. No, it's much simpler and yet much deeper than all that. Simply put, we are being pruned. Jesus is speaking about us and to us when he says,

> I am the true vine, and my Father is the vinegrower. He removes every branch in me that bears no fruit. Every branch that bears fruit he prunes to make it bear more fruit . . . I am the vine, you are the branches. Those who abide in me and I in them bear much fruit, because apart from me you can do nothing. (John 15:1–2, 5)

The church in the United States is being pruned in order to bear more fruit.

As I'm sure you know, but just to be official, pruning is a horticultural practice in which parts of a plant are removed to help improve or maintain health, reduce risk from falling branches, and to increase the yield or quality of flowers and fruits.[1] Jesus says the branches that bear no fruit at all are removed, but those that bear fruit will be pruned in order to bear more. We can take some comfort in the fact that we are being pruned. That means that we, the church, do actually bear fruit, but God is preparing us to bear more.

Which begs the question, "Exactly what fruit is Jesus talking about?" That's where we get into trouble. You see, we've confused the branches with the fruit over the course of the last seventeen centuries or so. Branches are a permanent part of the plant. They grow from the vine and always stay in the vine. The branches are the church, the people, the disciples. The fruit, on the other hand, can be picked, eaten, used for sustenance, and it is where the seeds are. Those seeds are meant to be cast, planted, tossed into the world.

Our mistake is that we've come to believe that our purpose as the church is to get as many branches as possible—sometimes at the expense of the fruit. We've been so deliberate about improving the status of the church that we've put the main purpose of the vine—the fruit—on hold. We've become more concerned about

---

1. *Wikipedia*, s.v. "pruning," http://en.wikipedia.org/wiki/Pruning.

the church (or at least our own parish or congregation) than we are about revealing God's mercy, compassion, love, forgiveness, and grace in the world. Paul wrote about the fruit of the Spirit to the Galatian churches: "The fruit of the Spirit is love, joy, peace, patience, kindness, generosity, faithfulness, gentleness, and self-control" (Gal 5:22–23). This is the purpose of the church: to bear the fruit of the Spirit.

A vine that has too many branches compared to the amount of fruit it produces isn't healthy. It cannot effectively do what it was planted to do. In order to help the vine bear the fruit it is intended to bear, it must be pruned. As the vine grower, God is pruning the church to restore our health and to allow us to be about God's purpose in planting the vine in the first place. It's much more about the fruit and a lot less about the branches. We've forgotten our purpose. We need the vine grower to restore us. We need pruning. And God is accomplishing it. This isn't an indictment of large churches with lots of branches. It's a perspective on the whole church—including each congregation—regarding the fruit produced by the church.

This is a book to help the North American church reclaim its identity as the body of Christ. We are created and equipped to bear the fruit of the reign of God in the world. Centered in the cross and resurrection of Jesus, the church exists to be the experts at forgiveness, compassion, love, mercy, and generosity, and to boldly live those things in the very midst of the world. That's a different emphasis than numerical growth.

To that end, and in the image of the divine Trinity, congregations of the church are called to enter into relationships within their neighborhoods. That's how God has worked throughout human history, and therefore is how the church is to operate as well. This book is written to help us reclaim that relational identity, guide us into the neighborhood, and reveal the reign of God already present there; that which we were created to do in the first place.

Introduction

IN THE EARLY SEVENTEENTH century, Galileo Galilei's support of Copernicanism rubbed everyone the wrong way because virtually all philosophers, theologians, and astronomers agreed as truth that the Earth is at the center of the universe. After 1610, when he began publicly advocating this *heliocentric* view which placed the sun at the center of the universe, he met with bitter opposition from pretty much every expert, who eventually denounced him to the Roman Inquisition early in 1615. In February 1616, the Church condemned *heliocentrism* as "false and contrary to Scripture,"[2] and Galileo was warned to abandon his support for it, which he promised to do. When he later defended his views, he was tried by the Inquisition, found "vehemently suspect of heresy," forced to recant, and spent the rest of his life under house arrest. Wow. That's what can happen when you challenge assumed truths.

But sometimes the assumed realities need questioning. In the church, we've operated with some of the same starting points and common agreements for so long that we no longer question them. They have become assumed truths. We rarely wonder about them anymore. And we've come to operate under them as if they were absolute.

2. Sharratt, *Galileo*, 127–31.

TWO FOUNDATIONALLY ACCEPTED BUT NONETHELESS MYTHICAL TRUTHS

In this book it is important to lift up and challenge two of these assumed truths. The first is how we measure *church success*. The other, very related to it, deals with the *goal of autonomy*. In this writing I hope, partially, to question and expose those assumed truths as myths. But more importantly, I hope to help congregations operate more clearly from God's call instead of culturally and ecclesiologically (fancy word for *how the church functions*) accepted mythological truths.

Because my work in this book challenges some of the very basic assumptions we make about our purpose as church, any congregational changes that result will likely be deep, and therefore probably slow ones. This is no quick-fix book! Don't worry if it takes time.

I hope you consider the possibilities. Our participation in God's vision is at stake. I think it's that important. Get your congregational leadership (or judicatory leadership) on board, get a team of five or six committed people together, and take some time with this. Just because there are some operating points for the church on which most everyone agrees doesn't mean we can't (or shouldn't) question them. Or at least talk about them. So be part of the conversation. Seek the direction, movement, and breath of the Holy Spirit. Then decide for yourself.

The Mythical Truth of Church Success

How do you measure success in the church, especially in the neighborhood congregation? In my denomination we fill out annual parochial reports, which reveal member gains (or losses), worship attendance increases (or decreases), a larger (or smaller) budgets, and so on. Good, measureable numbers. Solid. Up or down. Growth or decline. And—the message becomes readily apparent—success or failure.

We talk about congregations with increasing numbers of people and dollars as models for the rest of the church to follow, and we spend considerable time in print and in attitude trying to figure out the secret to this "kingdom of God" achievement. In contrast, the congregations that maintain similar numbers over the last five years are referred to as "stagnant," and those whose numbers are more than five percent lower are "in decline." These are hardly complementary descriptions. Who wants to be called "stagnant" or "in decline"? Because we assume bigger equals more successful, our effort and energy go into the numbers of attendees, members, and dollars received. Good, tangible, measurable success that we've all agreed to.

So what's wrong with this picture? Nothing, if you buy into a business model of success. You know the catchphrases: bigger is better, if you're not growing you're dying, stuff like that. But is that all there is to God's mission? Is God's vision for creation measured in such detached terms?

Let's face it; bigger is the "truth," the culturally accepted measure of success for pretty much everything. Sales, clients, market shares, bank accounts, properties, listeners, viewers, revenue streams, billable hours, and yes, even church members. I don't know about you, but that doesn't seem to nestle into Jesus' life, ministry, or teaching quite as comfortably as I had always assumed. Love God, love your neighbor—including your enemies. Sell your property and give the money to the poor. The last shall be first. Humans do not live by bread alone. One's life does not consist in the wealth of possessions. And then there's the whole cross thing: what was accepted by everyone as an absolute and utter defeat was the crowning glory in the reign of God. On and on, you can pick the texts. Jesus came proclaiming the presence of the long-awaited reign of God. Those with eyes to see it, will. Those with ears to hear it, will.

Don't get me wrong, there's nothing wrong with growth. We are, of course, to invite people into communities that reveal the reign of God. We are to participate in God's mission in the world, sharing the good news of forgiveness, hope, and life, and bidding others to be part of that mission too. But I'm calling into question the primary—and sometimes the only—successful standard of being the body of Christ as the number of hash marks in the "new member" column. In what ways can you numerically report love, mercy, compassion, and grace incarnated through relationships in the neighborhood? Where is the column that is set aside to check the number of times that forgiveness was freely given and relationships restored? How do you measure lives changed by the power of the gospel? How do you categorize the movement of the Holy Spirit?

If our energy is funneled into numerical growth in order to appear culturally successful, it probably isn't going into joining what God is up to in the neighborhood in order to be missionally successful. The neighborhood isn't put around the church in order to bolster the church's numbers. Rather, the church is placed in the neighborhood to reveal the vision of God, proclaim it, and join in its activity already there. Numerical growth may or may not be related to that, so it ought not be the primary measure of success.

Congregational rate of growth has little to do with being equipped to participate in missional relationships in the neighborhood. This might be good news for congregations that get beat up on their parochial reports. Some so-called "stagnant" and "declining" congregations might actually be more successful in God's mission than the neighborhood's fast-growing church. Of course, declining numbers certainly aren't any sort of measure of missional success either. It's just that the principal question can't be how many new members have joined the church, but how the church has joined God's mission of care and reconciliation. It can't be how many of them have joined us, but how many of us have joined them, and how the relationships that developed revealed the reign of God in their midst.

Being clear about who God is and what God is doing (and trying to do), and then finding ways to proclaim, point out, and participate with God need to be the standard in missional success. The assumed myth of numerical growth can no longer be trusted. Success in the church is not the number of chairs used in the worship space on an average Sunday.

The Mythical Truth of Autonomy

This second accepted myth runs even deeper. The agreement on this one is even more foundational in our understanding. I'm talking about the mythological agreement that autonomy, the ability to take care myself/ourselves, is desirable—even necessary—for individuals, congregations, and communities.

Let me show you how this plays out in a concrete way. Congregations virtually always want to serve, right? We organize ourselves around this understanding, establish practices to enhance this understanding, and speak openly about the ways in which we serve our communities. We make serving part of our mission statements. We put in on banners. We utilize it as a theme for our conferences and assemblies. Serving our world is often at the heart of our missional self-understanding (how we understand our purpose). Our understanding and view of Scripture justifies this starting point. We no longer question the truth of the assumption that we are here to serve. We speak of Jesus entering the world to serve the world, even to the point of dying for us. We, in turn, understand our role—our identity—in a similar fashion. We exist to serve the world, and in so doing hope to reveal Christ through our service. Does this sound about right so far? Keep going.

The common agreement that the church is here to serve is often the starting point when the church develops relationships with our neighbors. We ask who in our neighborhood needs help, who is hurting, who needs to be served? The answers to these questions are largely the basis for launching into relationships— relationships that allow our congregations to serve. We seek out the poor, the hungry, the homeless, and the disadvantaged. We support, supply, and partner with agencies and institutions in our communities that share our concern for the needy people in our neighborhoods. We do what we need to do in order to serve those who need our help.

How can anyone find fault with that, we ask? How can this accepted truth come into question? As sincere and good as this orientation of service is, it actually limits us. When we begin with the assumed truth that we are primarily "here to serve," doesn't that include having the resources necessary to serve? If we are to serve the poor, don't we need to have enough financial resources to give money away? If we are to serve the hungry, don't we need to have excess food to share? If we are to serve the spiritually searching, mustn't we have our theological ducks in a row? Well, at least the pastor does. Consistent with and informed by an American culturally assumed truth of serving, the starting point for many congregations is the acquisition of resources. We feel a need to make sure there is at least enough to sustain ourselves and then consider those we seek to serve. Serving requires the acquisition of extra resources before you can serve. In other words, having autonomy is having a position of power. You need me because I have what you need.

This starting place of serving is accepted as truth, but have you thought about how limiting that can be? Our core Christian doctrine of the Trinity, God in three persons whose very identity is derived from this triune relationship and mutual self-giving, is the opposite of autonomy. It's really not boring—you'll see in chapter 1. Authentic relationship, as the triune God reveals, is not defined in service only, but through genuine bonds where congregations both serve and are served. To only serve is to enter into relationships from a position of power rather than mutuality and reciprocity. "We are here to serve" actually means we are striving for autonomy, that we are striving not to need anyone or anything. Not a good definition of relationship. And that's the opposite of the nature of God, and therefore must also be the opposite of the purpose of the church.

Jesus models "autonomy-not" within his culture by both serving and being served. Anthony Gittins points this out, "For Jesus, the solution to the problem of hierarchy and dominance was to be both master and servant, both one up and one down, both host and guest, both stranger and host."[3] Several biblical stories reveal Jesus welcoming—even requesting—service from those around him. The woman who anointed Jesus with the expensive

3. Gittins, *Ministry at the Margins*, 147.

ointment of pure nard (Mark 14:3–9), the boy who offers his lunch of fish and loaves (John 6:8-9), and Jesus' request that his three closest disciples stay awake with him during his most difficult hour at Gethsemane (Matt 26:36–45) exemplify this. Jesus was not autonomous, but approached ministry from the perspective of relationship and sharing resources.

HOW TO USE THIS RESOURCE

Now that these two mythical truths are exposed, it's time to consider how to use this book. By the way, I use the word "congregation" a lot in this book, but I don't mean that as an exclusive term. Each time I use the word "congregation," please simply insert the term most appropriate for your circumstances. I mean the term as inclusive of parish, gathering, meeting, house church, faith community, ministry organization, judicatory, and so on.

Let me tell you how I intended this to go when putting this all together. This wasn't written to be read like a novel, cover-to-cover, in front of the fireplace with a glass of cabernet. Rather, this is a group workbook. Each chapter ends with discussion questions and action steps. Move through each chapter separately, working through the discussion and follow-up steps before moving on. I can't emphasize enough that many of the action steps request utilizing more people in your congregation. This is important! Gathering more people as you go not only honors the gifts of other people in your church, allowing their gifts to be recognized and used, but it creates more congregational buy-in as you move through.

You should begin by perusing the whole book. Consider the possibilities in your own congregation. Do the emphases make sense to you? Can you see this working in your place? And, are you the one who should take the lead in getting this going in your congregation? If not, can you identify such a person? Give this book to that person with your comments on it. If you're a pastor in the congregation, know that like it or not, you must lend your support if clarity of your congregation's purpose is to happen. If you're not the pastor (or not the lead pastor), that's one person who needs to be on board before anyone else. I don't necessarily think it ought to be that way, but it is. Let's deal with reality: pastors can sink a big project faster than a politician can throw blame. Or, as is unfortunately more often the case, pastors can passively-aggressively ignore something until it withers and dies on its own. Don't let that happen! Explain why you think this resource is a good idea, and offer to take the lead on it or find the appropriate person to do so. A pastor doesn't have to be on the team, though it's certainly better if she/he is. Even so, she/he doesn't have to take the lead, but definitely needs to be visibly and vocally supportive of the effort.

If you decide this is worth attempting in your congregation, get official permission from whatever governing entity necessary to enter into this process. No games here. No hidden agendas. No manipulation. Be absolutely honest and open about what you see in here and the hope you have for your congregation. They may decide to say no. Take that risk because it won't happen without their buy-in. Transparency and trust are key as you walk through these chapters. As you go through it, make sure you are open about the process. Again, look for ways to involve as many congregational members as you can along the way. Share your work and your findings thoroughly with each step of the journey. Over-communicating your discoveries will become a key factor in your progress.

Next, with clergy buy-in and leadership approval, pull together a team of five or six other people as the "Neighborhood Church Task Force" or whatever you want to call it. Make it at least five so that you have enough perspectives to be viable and can operate if someone misses a meeting; no more than eight so that the team is manageable, especially on those occasions when everyone actually shows up.

Make sure they know what they're committing to—again, no games or hidden agendas. Transparency is important at every step. Let them know that this is an effort to help your congregation be more open to God's activity in the world, that they will likely be recommending to the congregational leadership some significant changes, and that it may take a full year or more to work through— depending on what you hear and see along the way. Make sure these are team players, good listeners, open to change, spiritually mature, and willing to be patient during this journey. Or, barring that, just get the best people you can. Commit to meeting monthly, and sometimes more often when needed. Commit to sharing openly together as trust will become imperative. Make sure that everyone understands that personal agendas and preconceived notions, though unavoidable, will not be helpful. This is a time to listen to God, to one another, to the church, and to the neighborhood. New things will emerge, and your team needs to move with the Holy Spirit as that is recognized.

Finally, go for it. Get every team member a copy of this book and start. Enjoy the journey. Let me know how it goes.

Abbreviations

ARDA	Association of Religious Data Archives
ELCA	Evangelical Lutheran Church in America
LDS	The Church of Jesus Christ of Latter-Day Saints
NRSV	New Revised Standard Version of the Bible

1

The Nature and Mission of God

WE START WITH GOD. One basic assumption most Christians
have is that we know God. OK, we don't usually claim to know
everything about God, but we know the significant things. Father,
Son, Holy Spirit. Creator, Redeemer, Sanctifier. Forgiving, merci-
ful, compassionate. Loves us enough to send the Son who died on
the cross. Rose from the dead on the third day. Fills believers with
the Holy Spirit and empowers them for ministry. You know, the
important stuff. And, of course, I'm sure you can add more things
to the list that are foundational to you.

We generally use the same basic adjectives over and over to
describe God. We lift up biblical images and attach them to what
we already know. We become familiar with these basic descriptors,
then rarely go much deeper because, after all, who can really know
an infinite God? We don't usually spend a lot of time in the church
going into much more than these basics because we're all pretty
sure we know this stuff anyway.

Can you guess where I'm going here? Let me ask you: have
you ever taken part in a study or discussion about who God is?
This isn't a rhetorical question; I'm actually asking. It can be quite
enlightening to open up some of the presuppositions we bring to

the table when thinking about God. In my research for this book, I met with a church whose leaders spent almost a year and a half meeting monthly for the express purpose of trying to understand who God is. They went through quite a bit of the Bible in that time and paid special attention to passages, stories, and themes that showed God in a different light than they were used to or comfortable with. Their preconceived notions about the nature of God were exposed and a scriptural witness began to shape their understanding in different ways. Some of these ways were challenging; some were comforting. But one revelation that emerged during this time together was surprising to them: *the nature of God is primarily relational.*

Though they were excited by this understanding which led to some changes in their purpose, values, and organization, it really wasn't new. What they had discovered actually dates back to John of Damascus in the early eighth century AD, and is referred to as "perichoresis."

GOD ON "DANCING WITH THE STARS"

The term *perichoresis* in describing God was used by John of Damascus in his development of the doctrine of the Trinity. Perichoresis is a word used to "capture the mutual indwelling of the equal divine persons: Father, Son, and Spirit. The divine persons embrace one another in love and exist in one another."[1] What's more, it is either a noun or as a verb: "The noun means 'whirl or rotation,' the verb means 'going from one to another, walking around, handing around (for example, a bottle of wine, or of cola if you prefer), encircling, embracing, or enclosing."[2] OK, that's for you academic types.

That's a pretty good definition and quite thorough. But how about a less complicated image? The word *perichoresis* is made up of two parts: *peri,* meaning around, like the *peri*meter of a circle;

---

1. Moltmann, "Perichoresis," 113–14.
2. Ibid., 113.

and *choresis*, the basis of English words such as *choreography*, or moving together, specifically dancing together. Put them together, and you get "dancing around together"; a little bit of a stretch, but not completely off base.

Picture your favorite couple in "Dancing with the Stars." Admit it, you've watched it. How many of those fancy steps could happen if each partner didn't know what the other was doing—and trusted the other to do it? That kind of dancing can only happen because there is a relationship between partners. Through hours and hours of intensive practice, each partner comes to know the strengths and weakness of the other, and their own role in the dance is shaped by these. There would be nothing but sprains, bruises, broken limbs, or worse if there wasn't a trusting relationship between the partners. The dance routine both creates and expresses a reliance on the other. It's the trust, the reliance, the being shaped by the partner that gives the dance its unique artistic expression. That is also included in the meaning of perichoresis: trust, reliance, being shaped by the other.

Like partners in an intricate dance, each person of the Holy Trinity's steps and movements only make sense in relationship to the steps and movements of the others. It is in relationship, in *perichoretic mutuality*, that God exists as God. More than a way of behaving or a choice that is made, this relationship is the very *nature* of God. This relational nature is what theologians throughout the centuries have tried to articulate in the writings and doctrines of the church. In the Apostles' and Nicene Creeds, the church confesses its faith in a triune God. As Father, Son, and Spirit, God lives in community, God exists as a Trinity, in perichoretic relationship—each person of the Trinity in relationship with the others. Each person of the Trinity's identity is revealed in their relationship to the others.

The writer of the Gospel of John seems to get the nature of this relationship, "Even though you do not believe me, believe the works, so that you may know and understand that the Father is in me and I am in the Father" (John 10:38), and again,

> Do you not believe that I am in the Father and the Father
> is in me? The words that I say to you I do not speak on
> my own; but the Father who dwells in me does his works.
> Believe me that I am in the Father and the Father is in
> me; but if you do not, then believe me because of the
> works themselves. (John 14:10–11)

Each person of the Trinity is defined by, in service to, and in relationship with the others. God is God *as* community.

MISSIO DEI AND THE KINGDOM OF GOD

That's all well and good, but so what? Now we know a fancy word, *perichoresis*, and can impress our friends with our scholastic description of the Trinity (the "Dancing with the Stars" comparison notwithstanding). Perhaps now we even understand the nature of the triune God as self-giving relationship, but big deal. What does that have to do with helping my congregation become more successful in fulfilling our purpose? That's what we're reading this for, after all! Keep reading because, oh yes, there's more.

If the triune God *is* perichoretic relationship and therefore *is* trust, reliance, and being shaped by the other, then we who are created in the image of God are primarily relational beings too. We are not fully human when we exist alone. We need not only a relationship with God, but with other people too. Even the most introverted of us cannot function without other people. It's part of what it means to be human. The deeper and more trusting our relationships, the more we are reflecting the image of God in which we are created. What that means is that rather than striving for personal autonomy and independence, the godly thing to do is to live in more significant relationships. How empty it would be to trust no one, to accomplish everything alone. What a sad existence it would be if we had no one to give ourselves to, no one to serve, no one whose very presence helps shape our identity. This is perichoresis, and it is the image of God.

God *as* relationship means that everything God does has a mutual, relational, perichoretic nature to it. Not around the edges of God's activity, but at the very heart of who God is and all God does. The opening verses of Genesis reveal that it was out of relational love, creativity, and selflessness that God poured forth light and dark, sea and land, plant and animal (Gen 1 and 2). When sin and death entered God's good world through human beings and annulled the relationship God had established with the world (Gen 3), God made a commitment to redeem this beloved creation and restore the relationship. God has been acting on that commitment ever since. This is the *missio Dei*, or mission of God. The heart of God's ongoing activity in the world is the restoration of relationship.

David Bosch supports this idea of *missio Dei* as, "God's involvement in and with the world, the nature and activity of God, which embraces both the church and the world, and in which the church is privileged to participate."[3] In other words, God can't leave us alone. It would be contrary to the very nature of who God is to not be involved with us, committing every relational resource available to win us back. And this obviously can't be done by force, manipulation, or command. That wouldn't be very relational, after all. No, God goes about the business of restoring relationship in a, well, relational sort of way.

Haven't you wondered why God doesn't just snap divine fingers and make the world right, cure disease, solve hunger, bring peace, and alleviate injustice? Have you ever thought that God should maybe be more *efficient*? Why does God allow poverty, war, tragedy, and disaster to continue? These are certainly complex issues that the best theologians throughout the ages have been unable to resolve adequately. My own contribution to this conversation is that the standard we set for God is *our* agenda, not God's. God is much more concerned about the relationship of creation than the perceived efficiency of it. And as hard to swallow as that may be at times, we've got to remember that if we disagree with God, one of us is wrong. Guess who?

Apparently the relational approach—since it is God's—is the godliest one. Consider that every time God does something

3. Bosch, *Transforming Mission*, 10.

significant in biblical history, God always seems to do it via a relationship of some sort. Why else would God go to all the trouble of saving a portion of creation with Noah when God could have much more efficiently simply started over? Wouldn't it have been more impressive for God to instantly create a nation of *God's people* in a convincing fashion than to begin with the lying and laughing Abraham and Sarah? Wouldn't it have been more spectacular to lead the enslaved Hebrews from captivity in Egypt via some sort of molecular-level transporter, à la Star Trek, instead of working with the weak, murdering, stuttering Moses? Each time, God chooses to establish a relationship with someone or some group and accomplish God's purposes with them. The nature of God, and therefore of those created in that image, is always relationship.

Nowhere is this seen more clearly and accomplished more fully than on the cross. Central to God's reconciling work is Jesus Christ. It is in Jesus that God's fullest self-revelation is accomplished, and that the possibility of restored relationship most fulfilled. Jesus came in the vulnerability of relationship: born as a baby into a poor family. His ministry on earth was spent in developing close relationships with disciples, the least likely twelve becoming his friends. Much of his time was spent relationally: touching, healing, teaching, and even partying. In Jesus, God's redemptive and relational mission was revealed to the world in an example hard to dismiss. Through the work of the Spirit of the crucified and risen Jesus, people in all cultures are brought into a relationship with God. This is the work of the Holy Spirit active in each culture, including our own neighborhood, and the church is created and called to reveal and participate in it.

FOR DISCUSSION:

1. What is your earliest "memory" of what God looks like? Where do you think this image came from? How has this first image influenced you as you've grown and matured in your faith?

2. Review the idea of *perichoresis* as trust, reliance, and being shaped by the other. Think of "Dancing with the Stars" where each partner needs the other in order to do their own steps. Talk for a few minutes about how this relates to God as three-in-one.

3. As a follow-up discussion on *perichoresis*, how is your own identity shaped by the close relationships you have?

4. As people created in the image of God, what does *perichoresis* reveal about our personal identity? How might it help us understand the identity of the church?

5. How do you feel about God's choice to accomplish very important things in the world through relationships with less-than-perfect human beings?

6. How significant is it that God chooses relationships over efficiency in bringing the vision of God into the world?

2

The Purpose of the Church

HERE'S A QUICK REVIEW:

- God as Trinity means that each person of the Holy Trinity finds his/her identity in a self-giving relationship with the others (perichoresis).

- The essence of God is relationship, so God's activity and mission are based in relationship.

- We are created in God's image, and therefore are most human in trusting, genuine relationships.

- God's primary mission activity in the world (*missio Dei*) is the redeeming and restoring of the world's relationships to one another and to God.

- God historically advances that mission primarily through relationships with particular people or groups of people.

- This mission is revealed and takes place fully in the life, ministry, death, and resurrection of Jesus.

The next questions, then, are these: if God is doing all this, and has accomplished it so fully for the sake of the world in Jesus, then why does the church exist? What's our role, our purpose? How do we go about it?

As the church, we've made assumptions about the answers to these questions over the centuries, and as often as not have been wrong. One reason is that we tend to start by looking at the church first—beginning by trying to figure out our purpose and role. Only *after* that do we spend any significant time looking for God. The problem is that we've already created church-oriented filters through which we will see God. When you think about this, it's really quite backwards, and limits our perception on the purpose of the church.

For instance, when we start with our purpose before we consider what God is doing, we often assume a particular structure for the church. Beginning with a board, we have committees or teams and then look for God to work within that structure. Or perhaps we would start with the assumption that because we are a church, we need a choir, a pipe organ, Sunday School, Confirmation, and other standard church accouterments. Once these are firmly entrenched, we seek God's presence in these things and pray those involved will be spiritually filled and enriched, asking God to bless our efforts.

Now I'm not trying to open a can of worms here, nor am I saying these things aren't necessarily helpful. The God who created the universe and all that it contains certainly uses churches that start with themselves too. I'm merely pointing out that in many ways we're driving in reverse by *starting* with the church, and only *after* that considering God. Though in this work we will make other mistakes, we won't make that one. We spent the entirety of chapter 1 considering God. Now, with that foundation, we can consider the church.

LISTENING TO GOD IS NEVER COMPLETE

Knowing all sorts of things *about* God won't do much good without recognizing the current activity of God, right here, right now. God is certainly not static or complacent, but has a mission to be about, and is accomplishing it—doing so right now as you read this.

It's imperative, therefore, that we do our best to keep up with what God is doing. That requires paying attention to God and God's activity. And that involves listening to God so we can recognize God's mission activity and join in when we see it.

Listening to God as a spiritual discipline is an ongoing way of life. It's never completed, so instead we say, "I'm not there yet, but I'll move forward with what I've got." Listening to our neighbors is also an ongoing struggle that we'll never quite accomplish. But we can't wait until we feel completely competent or expert, otherwise we'll continue to sit still. Learning and growing won't do any good if we merely sit on the knowledge. With each new gain in experience and growth, we then go about these things more fully. And then more fully yet. And then even more fully after that. We continue to grow and struggle and recognize mistakes and grow some more. We never arrive at perfect listening, yet by the same token we also need to begin.

I'm convinced that the only real failure is failing to try. One thing we need to get over is the fear of making mistakes. Will we ever know God fully? Of course not! But we can recognize God doing some things, and can respond accordingly. That doesn't mean we don't continue to grow in our understanding of who God is and what God is about, but we still follow as we are able. Today. And then tomorrow. And then the next day.

I understand that sometimes the newness of growth can be frightening—even to the point of paralysis. A new insight into how God works may force us to reinterpret pretty much everything we thought we knew about God. Excellent! How exciting is that? And yet, instead of reveling in the work of the Spirit making all things new, we throw our spiritual gearshifts into *park* for fear of having to reevaluate all our previous activity and motivations. Reinterpretation with new awareness is part of the journey. It doesn't devalue what's gone on before, the listening we've previously done, or the discipleship activity in which we've been engaged. It simply means that there'll be a new twist to it now based on different insights.

And then new twists after that. And then more after that. Rather than being signs of mistakes or failures, these are signs of the living Christ who brings light and life.

Enjoy the journey. Make the mistakes. Recognize the successes. Learn and grow and follow. Listen with the ears you have now. And tomorrow listen with the ears you have tomorrow. I wonder if this is partly what the author meant when writing to the Hebrew Christians, "Let us run with perseverance the race that is set before us, looking to Jesus the pioneer and perfecter of our faith" (Hebrews 12:1–2). We simply continue. Not perfectly; sometimes crawling at a snail's pace. But we move and act on what we have, seeking the voice of God and neighbor again tomorrow. We'll never get it perfectly, folks. As Martin Luther wrote to Philipp Melanchthon in August of 1521,

> Be a sinner and sin boldly, but believe and rejoice in Christ even more boldly. For he is victorious over sin, death, and the world. As long as we are here we have to sin. This life in not the dwelling place of righteousness but, as Peter says, we look for a new heavens and a new earth in which righteousness dwells . . . Pray boldly; you too are a mighty sinner.[1]

HOW ARE YOU DOING WITH SPIRITUAL DISCIPLINES?

Let's not assume anything: how's your team's prayer life? Here's a pretty good litmus test: pray out loud together. Well, one at a time, but with everybody participating. How comfortable are you with this? Is your comfort or discomfort related to your confidence in prayer? This isn't to put anyone on the spot, but it is a way that your team can be helpful to one another in developing prayer.

Do each of you study Scripture regularly? Are all of you part of a Bible study in your congregation? The Bible is a primary way in which God comes to us. It makes it hard to be listening to God

1. Luther, *Letters 1*, 281–82.

in general if we aren't listening to God in one of the specific ways God has promised to be present. As you gather as a team, spend some time in Scripture together. Discover things about God you may not have known before. Feel free to use the "Foundation for Mission Bible Study" in appendix A, following one session each time you meet.

Are you all in corporate worship every week? And, if your church body is sacramental in nature, do you participate in holy communion as often as it is offered? Gathering together as a worshiping community is integral to listening. Sunday morning (or whenever your congregation gathers for worship) is likely the safest place to listen to God; everyone's there to do the same thing. You've got the "two or three gathered in [Jesus'] name" (Matt 18:20), you've got Scripture, you've got sacraments, you've got the community of believers, you've got singing, and you've got the promise of God to be present. This is the very stuff of listening to God! Take advantage of this. Make sure you're not just present in corporate worship, but active in corporate worship.

Don't get itchy here, but how's your financial giving? I've told those in new member classes that if they want a fast and simple way to grow deeper spirituality, start tithing (giving away 10 percent of your income) right now. It's simple, but not easy for most. And yet it is a deeply important spiritual thing to do. Giving away a significant amount of money, especially through your congregation's offering plate, does a few things: It helps you recognize that money is a way to work with God and not just a goal for security. It expresses where you place your trust. It helps you participate with God in revealing God in the world. It is tangible evidence that money is not the lord of your life.

I heard someone say one time that giving isn't about what it can do for God, since God certainly doesn't need your money. Rather, it's what giving can do for you. It is a spiritual discipline, on par with prayer, holy communion, baptism, and the Bible. Don't neglect this one.

BEYOND INDIVIDUAL PRACTICES

I know some congregations that have each declared a "Sabbath Year." All major decisions were put on hold, anything that would alter the course of the congregation was tabled, and the whole congregation spent a full year learning and practicing listening to God. They did this in every way you can imagine. Classes, retreats, vigils, forums, sermons, walks, yoga, music, writing, sharing in groups, painting, and more. They spent about half the year teaching one another and practicing how to listen to God, and the other half of the year continuing to practice and sharing with one another what they were hearing.

It took some work and some dedication, but amazing things came about as a result. These congregations became better equipped for listening not only to God, but to one another, and to their neighbors. They were able to move forward with confidence that they were sailing with the wind of the Holy Spirit.

Since listening and relationship-development are time-consuming processes, I'd encourage you to take congregational time to set apart for listening. Declare a time of Sabbath. Try it for a full year so that it has time to sink in with everyone. If a year seems out of reach, make it at least several months. Using this book in conjunction with a time of Sabbath would be a dynamic way to grow in spirituality, listening, and relationship.

In short, make sure that doing your best to listen to God becomes a way of life. Honestly, unless that's happening, the rest of what you'll read here will be pointless. God is doing some pretty amazing stuff right now in your neighborhood. It's worth your time to know God better so you can point it out, proclaim it, and participate in it.

THE CHURCH IN THE IMAGE OF GOD

We know that the triune God is a God of relationship, mutuality, and transparent love for the sake of the other. This is essential to the nature of God. It is core, foundational, and basic. Each person of the Trinity finds her/his fullest identity in relationship with the others. That is God. This is seen most clearly in Jesus, whose incarnation reveals God's nature in ways we can grasp best. No one expressed this self-giving nature-of-God-in-Jesus more clearly than the Apostle Paul in his letter to the Philippian church,

> Let the same mind be in you that was in Christ Jesus, who, though he was in the form of God, did not regard equality with God as something to be exploited, but emptied himself, taking the form of a slave, being born in human likeness. And being found in human form, he humbled himself and became obedient to the point of death—even death on a cross. (Phil 2:5–8)

As Jesus, God the Son emptied himself into the world for the sake of the world. In becoming part of the created world God loves so deeply, God has been influenced and informed by the world in intimate ways. That's what happens in relationships. Rather than being *ungodly*, it was the only *godly* thing to do (perichoretic nature of God, remember?). The Christian church, the body of Christ, has at the foundation of its identity this same nature of loving relationship. It follows, then, that local congregations, as neighborhood expressions of Christ's church, recognize who they are and what that identity means in their neighborhoods.

Congregations, in order to be most fully the church, are intimately involved in and with their neighborhoods. The neighborhood is changed by the presence of a Christian congregation in their midst. Change experienced by the neighborhood through its relationship to the local congregation may in fact reveal the *missio Dei* at work, enfleshed by the church.

But relationships go both ways. When a congregation is in relationship with its neighborhood, the church won't remain the same either. To expect influence to go only one direction is a form of autonomy, a seeking of power, and reveals a lack of a true relationship. Unless a congregation is willing to be changed by its neighborhood by entering into mutual relationship there, it isn't really revealing the perichoretic nature of God. Change experienced by the congregation may truly clarify the activity of God already going on in the neighborhood. The *godliness* of a congregation is more deeply known in relationships. These changes in both neighborhood and congregation, as assessed through Scripture, discernment of the Spirit's direction by the congregation, and the historical views of the church, can help reveal the Spirit of God at work.

Congregations are created in this same relational image, in relationship with God, one another, and the world. Created in the image of a perichoretic God, the church is called to have mutual and self-giving relationships not only among the members of the congregational community, but with the surrounding neighborhood beyond the congregation's membership. As God is active in the world, in relationship to the world, in service to the world, Christian congregations are created and called in the same identity.

CHALLENGING THE MYTH OF AUTONOMY

Since relationships, then, are so central to the purpose of the church, why do our congregations struggle so much with them? Why is a book like this one, helping us strengthen relationships in our neighborhoods, necessary?

Among the most prevalent spiritual forces of darkness in the United States are strict privacy and individualism. These are foremost in the mindset of modern and postmodern Western culture; and when you think about it, are in direct contradiction to the perichoretic, triune God. Because they are the opposite of the relational nature of God, these are among the powers of brokenness to which we all fall prey. That includes the church. Often in sincere efforts to be holy and godly, congregations attempt to set themselves apart from their neighbors in the neighborhood. When they believe they are a refuge from the world, congregations are actually doing the opposite of what they are attempting to do. Rather than revealing godliness to the neighborhood, congregations that ignore or neglect relationships within their neighborhoods exhibit the broken powers of individualism.

Again, when we put our primary energy into coercing or manipulating those in our neighborhoods to convert to our brand of Christianity, we are neglecting an "image of God" relationship with them. The gospel is much more about restoring relationships than it is about our perception of individual salvation. Isn't that in keeping with a perichoretic God whose very nature is relationship? Interesting, don't you think? This is good news for those who find evangelism terrifying. The Great Commission in Matthew 28, "Go therefore and make disciples of all nations, baptizing them in the name of the Father and of the Son and of the Holy Spirit, and teaching them to obey everything that I have commanded you," is fulfilled in trusting, self-giving relationships, not in theological debate or purity of doctrine.

The church, as the community created by God in the name of Jesus, is the community called and sent through the power of the Holy Spirit to reveal a new approach to the brokenness in the world. Congregations, though made up of broken and sinful people, are also a holy people redeemed in Jesus Christ. As part of a neighborhood, congregations enter into relationships within their neighborhoods, and in doing so, reveal and participate in God's redemptive activity centered in Christ on the cross.

THEOLOGY OF THE CROSS AS PART OF MISSIO DEI

In summarizing Martin Luther's concept of the theology of the cross from the *Heidelberg Disputation* of 1518, Kelly Fryer states:

> Luther reminds us that, while God could have come to us in all kinds of ways, God chose to come down here to meet us in the most unlikely place of all: on the cross, in the face of an outcast and a stranger, who suffered there and died. And God *had* to do this because we had made such a mess of things.[2]

This is the God who, in Jesus Christ, enters into a relationship with us while we are still in our sin, who meets us in our darkness, and who sticks with us when we are opposed to God.

2. Fryer, *Reclaiming the "L" Word*, 42.

This is the God who forgives, recreates, and makes new in Christ. As the church, the body of Christ, we are forgiven and made new not just for our own sakes, but in order to reveal forgiveness and new life to our neighborhoods. The perichoretic God of relationship is already present there, regardless of how secular, unholy, and disbelieving our communities may be. In the cross of Jesus, God is about the business of meeting us and the other people of our neighborhoods in our brokenness and bringing renewal.

As the church, met by God in the cross of Christ and made new in the Holy Spirit, we are created, called, and sent into our neighborhoods to live and proclaim this theology of the cross. Whether our neighborhoods are rich or poor, drug-infested or pristine, gay or straight, we and the people who live in our surrounding communities with us are broken, sinful, and hopeless. White, Black, Hispanic, Asian, Native American, Latino, or immigrant, all are far from God. "For by grace you have been saved through faith, and this is not your own doing; it is the gift of God— not the result of works, so that no one may boast" (Eph 2:8–9).

As the God of the cross reaches the people of our neighborhoods in their sin, shame, and brokenness, we are called to follow God there as well. Forgiven at the cross, we forgive those who live among us in our communities. Made new in Christ, we reveal new life in our neighborhoods. Met by God in our brokenness, sinfulness, and disbelief, we join God in meeting our neighbors in their brokenness, sinfulness, and disbelief. In those places, at those times, standing with our neighbors in loving relationship, we reveal the mercy we've been shown. We do this as friends, not as superiors; through relationships, not through arrogance; through mutual giving and receiving, not from a position of spiritual power.

RELATIONSHIP AND CONTEXT

In the person of Jesus, God the Son became human. In him, God has entered the creation as part of the creation. An infinite God became incarnate in the world, the Word of God became flesh (John 1:14).

Not only was Jesus born into the world, but was born into a particular context in a particular point in creation history. The customs, the language, the culture, the religious practices, and more were all part of Jesus' life and ministry. Even the manner in which he was killed—crucifixion—was a specific contextual practice. Not only did Jesus have a significant effect on the world, but the particulars of his neighborhood had a significant effect on him. In Jesus, God can be known, seen, and joined in the specifics of his community.

In the person of Jesus, God reveals that God's mission is for all people, in all times and all places. At the same time, he reveals the need for the body of Christ to be particular to our own context—our own neighborhood. Craig Van Gelder describes this ability of Jesus to be known and accepted as Messiah and Lord in any context as the "translatability of the gospel," and the necessity of the church to proclaim and participate with Jesus as Lord in all cultures as the "translatability of the church."[3] By becoming part of a particular culture for the sake of the whole world, Jesus has established that God is active in the specifics of any culture at any point in history. The incarnation of Christ reveals that God works in and through particular contexts.

Congregations exist in particular neighborhoods in specific points in history. Our members are part of the contexts of the neighborhood in which we live. The incarnation reveals that in order to live out our missional identity—and, in fact, form a missional identity—our congregations must be part of the contextual culture of our neighborhoods. As part of the body of Christ, congregations participate in the activity of God in our particular contexts. And as part of a particular context, we reveal this activity of God present in our neighborhoods. We must, in fact, be informed by our context as well as inform it. The triune God is the beginning and the source of a congregation's relationship with its neighborhood.

These attributes of God must, by definition, look different throughout the various periods of history and in the multitudes of

3. Van Gelder, *Missional Church in Context*, 33–34.

cultures that exist and have existed in this world. God, being God, meets every culture in the midst of its cultural context, entering into and relating from within each social environment as it exists. The perichoretic God is contextual, so God's missional activity within each culture is shaped by and helps shape the culture itself.

From the earliest scriptural witness to God's relationship with a broken humanity, God works within a specific context: "Then the eyes of both were opened, and they knew that they were naked; and they sewed fig leaves together and made loincloths for themselves . . . And the LORD God made garments of skins for the man and for his wife, and clothed them" (Gen 3:7, 21).

In covering themselves, these first humans reveal their shame and their separation from a relational God. They want more than the mutual relationship they had with God, instead wanting to be like God on their own terms. In the midst of this selfish betrayal, God meets them in their specific situation, and reveals care and love by ministering to their particular needs at the time. Rather than the clothes of fig leaves that humanity sewed together to cover their shame in separating themselves from God, God comes to them in the midst of their sin and shame, providing more protective, longer lasting, and probably less itchy clothes of animal skins. This ministerial act by God is specific to humanity's context at the time. Though I don't think many of us in our culture would welcome the gift of an animal-skin loincloth, for Adam and Eve it was absolute grace.

God works in the midst of our neighborhoods as they are now and meets the needs there, to be sure. More than working in the context, God enters the neighborhood itself, being shaped by it and redeeming it as a relational part of it. As stated above, the fullest example of this is Jesus himself, the Second Person of the triune God, who took on human flesh as part of creation (John 1).

The church, called and created in this image of God, does the same thing as it lives missionally. Congregations exist as part of specific neighborhoods. These neighborhoods in turn exist as part of a particular culture. The Christian church, the body of Christ, has as its very identity a nature of involvement in and with these neighborhoods in loving relationship. Our congregations, as neighborhood expressions of the church, need to have this understanding of who we are and what that identity means in our neighborhood.

Congregations are to gather in worship, be immersed in God's Word, participate regularly in sacraments, and practice disciplines of faith to be in positions of renewal by the Holy Spirit and to grow in a new life in Christ. But in order to most fully be the church, we must also be intimately involved in and with our neighborhoods. In our efforts to be godly, congregations sometimes attempt to remain isolated, insulated, and withdrawn; we try to become a fortress of righteousness separated from the unrighteous world around them. We can falsely consider ourselves a holy place in the midst of unholiness, a refuge from the sinfulness that fills the neighborhood in which we are placed.

The nature of God, however, denotes relationship within the existing context. The nature of the Trinity, the reality of God incarnate in Christ, the history of God's covenants with Israel, and God's acts of mercy and compassion maintain that relationships are integral to who God is and how God works in the world. Beginning with the triune God, the church is called to be in relationship with God, with one another, and with the world. This identity must therefore also be lived out in our congregation's relationship with our immediate neighborhood. Congregations are not to live in isolation, but in mutual relationship in and with our contexts. This is essential to our missional identity given by a missional God.

To reveal the reality of a gracious, forgiving, redeeming, and relational God in our neighborhood, to fulfill our purpose as part of God's mission, we need to be in relationship with our own neighborhood. In order to do that, we must get to know our neighborhood. That's the subject of the next chapter.

FOR DISCUSSION:

1. Does your congregation have a purpose statement? Do you know it? Does it contain any relationship language? How does it help you participate in God's mission?

2. Reflect on your congregation's relationships in your neighborhood. How is God's nature being revealed? How are your neighbors becoming aware of God's nature through you?

3. Can you identify anything going on in your congregation's neighborhood that reveals God's presence now? For example, are there agencies that help the poor, families that love foster children, or individuals that stand with those who are bullied? What can your church learn about God from these people?

4. Talk about how your spiritual disciplines (prayer, worship, Bible reading, generous giving) can help your ability to listen to God. How good a listener are you?

5. Have you heard God speak to you or to your congregation? If so, how did you know it was God? What did God say?

3

A Basis for Relationship with Your Neighbors—Listening

IT'S EVENING, AND YOU'RE finally settled at the dinner table. Just as the first spoonful of long-awaited yam and celery soup is approaching your mouth, the doorbell rings. You aren't expecting anyone, but you experience a sinking feeling in your stomach because you strongly suspect who it is. It's someone with an agenda that isn't yours but who will insist that their agenda become yours. Yes, it's someone selling something.

The single-pane aluminum frame windows in your house have been a virtual neon sign inviting every construction company and window pane producer in a five-state area to ring your bell. A recent hail storm has every roof inspector in existence descending on your neighborhood. The initiative on the next ballot will apparently affect your great-great grandchildren, either making or breaking their very lives. You will be condemned to an eternity of suffering unless you accept the religious message of the young zealots on your porch. Household break-ins are on the rise, and your only hope for securing your valuables—and maybe your life—is through signing a multiyear contract tonight with a particular home security company.

You know how it goes. These interruptions are annoying at best, and rarely have anything to do with your actual needs. Yet they keep coming. People come to your door uninvited and hope you will alter your schedule for them and their product. And they expect you to pay them for the privilege! There are even a few who will use high pressure, manipulative techniques, telling you things that may or may not be true just to get you sign on the dotted line tonight.

Not surprisingly, however, this is often how the residents of neighborhoods see local congregations. Our neighbors perceive a local congregation as yet one more entity primarily seeking its own profit and benefit. And, to be honest, there is good reason for that. As the church, we often are more concerned about selling *our* product than in being in relationship for the sake of our *neighbors*. We justify this by saying that what we are selling is exactly what they need. Whether or not that is true isn't the issue here. No one likes someone else's agenda imposed on them. Whether the church goes door-to-door or offers great youth programming, we are often correctly perceived as seeking to benefit ourselves, bolster our membership, fill our pews, and most importantly, increase our offering.

I know this sounds terribly cynical, but we need to be honest here. Isn't that how we measure our success as a congregation (see the section in the introduction called *The Mythological Truth of Church Success*)? Using the same primary criteria for success as someone selling faulty vacuum cleaners doesn't seem in keeping with the vision of God. It's time to challenge our assumptions about success. It's time to consider the reign of God before we consider the annual congregational report. It's time to put the needs of our neighbors ahead of the needs of our organization. It's time to strengthen relationships with our neighbors. It's time to reveal the perichoretic nature of God in our communities. And, like all relationships, this starts with listening.

Wouldn't it be nice if, instead of coming uninvited to sell a particular product—one you may or may not need or even want—there were caring and trustworthy people who actually had your best interests at heart? Not offering you *their* product to increase *their* sales commission, but helping *you*, listening to *you*, making *your* needs their priority? Can you imagine someone patiently taking the time to really learn what you wanted, what you needed, and only then sought to help you get it?

Yeah, right. That door-to-door company wouldn't last long. Yet that's really the point: the church isn't a door-to-door sales company.

Can we be the organization that takes the time to listen, to learn, to meet needs that emerge from relationships rather than the organization's agenda? Shouldn't the church be this? Relationship is the nature of the triune God, the God we are called and sent to reveal. Relationships, then, need to be our first priority as the church. Relationships involve trust. Trust takes time to develop. That, again, begins with listening.

LEARNING TO LISTEN

Developing significant relationships between individuals is time-consuming. No lifelong partnership can be deep and authentic overnight. What's more, the effort that goes into growing relationships is ongoing. You never reach a level at which you can say, "Finally, I've achieved it. A perfect relationship. No more listening required!" Hardly. Authentic listening is not only necessary to grow a relationship, it is deeply built in to a relationship. It is, in fact, a major part of defining a relationship.

If that is all true for individuals, it is even more so for entities or organizations. Though perhaps more complex and intricate, the same relationship principles apply. And yet, it is something we aren't necessarily good at. Most of us would prefer to tell our story rather than listen to someone else's, share our knowledge rather than learn from someone else. So this will require some committed effort on your part. It may seem awkward or even unnatural at first. But remember, it is necessary if we are to be a church that reveals the nature of God in our neighborhoods. Eventually you'll find your way and discover some wonderful ways to develop relationships in your congregation's broader community, but in the meantime, here are some pretty concrete ways to begin the process of listening to your neighborhood. The goal is to listen to *their* agenda, not put forth your own. Don't *sell* anything. Just listen. You may be quite surprised at what you hear.

Take a Walk

Not all listening is done with your ears. You can get some pretty good information about the needs, wants, desires, and priorities of your congregation's neighborhood just by looking at it. Take a walk through your neighborhood together. You'll probably have to do this on several evenings, breaking up the neighborhood into manageable regions. That's fine; you're not necessarily in a hurry. Another option would be to break up into separate teams of three or four people each. You can cover more territory, but you need to listen carefully to the other teams when you debrief. This is a good time to recruit a few others from your congregation to walk with you. Get their input and observations. And you also get better communication about your process and a broader buy-in to what you're doing.

Although you don't need to cover every square foot of the neighborhood, you really do need to spend time in different areas to get a feel for it. If some members of your team live in the neighborhood, they have to be quiet, or perhaps not even present, when you walk their vicinity. You want to get fresh and objective views, and someone on your team might bias the whole listening process through vocalizing their long-held perspectives.

As you walk, what do you notice about the buildings and properties that make up the homes, schools, businesses, pastures, open areas? Are they well-kept or shoddy? Old or new? Colorful or drab? What might that indicate? If there are taller buildings, be sure to look up at the architecture above. What is depicted or symbolized there? Are buildings built to honor or remember specific people? What is the mood that seems to be prevalent? Be sure to look at the sidewalks and streets. Are they broken and rough, or well taken care of? Are there fences? How tall are they? How well-kept are they? Can neighbors see each other through them or are they built for privacy? Make mental notes as you go, pointing things out to each other.

If you meet people on your walk, casually observe them, too. What age(s) are they? What color or nationality are they? Do they greet you or ignore you? Do you feel threatened or safe (be careful that you aren't projecting your own preconceived notions here)? Pay attention to who you *don't* see. Are there any children? Any teenagers? Any single people? Any gay couples? Any elderly? Any particular ethnic groups not in evidence? What and who you don't see may be as helpful as what and who you do.

Gather back together and share your observations. Make sure someone writes this stuff down; it'll be helpful later on. Talk together about themes that emerge. Is the whole neighborhood pretty homogenous or are there different areas with different atmospheres? What was surprising? What did you notice that everyone else noticed? What did you notice that was unique to you? Be careful you don't rush to any conclusions here; keep to actual observations. You're just starting to listen—let the process unfold on its own!

Host a Town Hall Meeting

Is there an issue or initiative that is presently burning locally? Something coming up in an election that is controversial? This can be a great opportunity to listen! Have your congregation host a town hall meeting with speakers from both sides. If there is a zoning issue for a new business, have someone from the local chamber of commerce come, along with someone from the environmental preservation group that is in opposition. Make sure the ground rules are clear and friendly. This is not to take sides, but to listen as well as to give your neighbors the opportunity to hear firsthand both sides of an issue. School bond referendum coming up? Have the principal of a local school or a school board member speak to the benefits, giving equal time to a representative of the homeowners association whose taxes will be raised.

Here's another chance to get more congregational members involved. Create an "Issue Town Hall" team or committee. Have them get speakers arranged well ahead of time. Then publicize, publicize, publicize. There's nothing worse than a town hall meeting with no one present. You'll have a hard time getting anyone to attend a second one, much less speak.

Make sure the moderator or facilitator is a good one. Perhaps there's someone gifted in that area from your congregation who can do it well. If so, then fine. Just be careful that whoever moderates this event is perceived as objective and fair. This person needs to be able to keep things moving and friendly. Depending on how hot the issue is, the moderator may need to be able to keep peace with some agitated attendees too. That's fine, just make sure everyone's clear beforehand as to the purpose and the agenda.

One word of caution here: your congregation's tax-exempt status may ride on the church not endorsing any political candidate or issue. Be very clear that this town hall meeting is for information only, and is not any type of endorsement. Make sure there are articulate representatives on both sides present with equal opportunity to speak and relay information. Sure, there can be questions and answers, but keep things civil. Remember, the goal is to listen, not to convince.

Survey (Be Careful!)

Often the first way we want to listen for information is the ever-present "conduct a survey" route. The idea is great: go door-to-door (see a problem emerging already?), asking residents some questions that will provide key information about the neighborhood. Although the concept is fine, the reality can prove more difficult if you really want it to be helpful. Anything that parallels "door-to-door" smells of an imposed agenda—an attempt to sell something. Unsolicited phone calls fall into this category also. Unless the homeowner knows the person who's knocking, they may not even answer the door. Or if they do, they might be suspicious as to your motives. Perhaps not, but it warrants some awareness in trying to get an accurate picture of the neighborhood. Another difficulty with surveys lies with the questions themselves. Some surveys are done with a particular outcome in mind, and the questions weighted toward that outcome, e.g., do you support *butterflies and rainbows that will result from "our" agenda* or do you support *torturing puppies that will result from "their" agenda?* Even though that obviously wouldn't be your tactic, sometimes we unwittingly lean one particular direction without intending to. And sometimes the questions we ask are interpreted differently by different people and therefore the feedback isn't as helpful as it could be.

The point being that although a survey can be a helpful tool, it needs to be done with more care and planning than most people think. If you believe a survey would help—and I'm not convinced it's the best way to listen—then go ahead. It can be helpful, but make sure it isn't the only tool in your listening toolbox. My recommendation would be to hire a professional survey group to work with you. They can help you clarify the information you're seeking, help you compose questions that will actually elicit that information, help you decide whether a phone survey or a mailed survey would work better, and help you identify who to survey and when to survey them so you get an accurate sampling of your neighborhood. They can be expensive, but you're much more likely to get information back that's worth listening to. Some companies will conduct the surveys for you, but that costs more yet.

If you choose to do a survey of the residents/workers in your neighborhood on your own, here are some things to consider:

- Utilize "SurveyMonkey.com" or a similar web-based survey guide. The basic plan is free, and they help you formulate questions that can get you the most helpful results.

- Make sure you survey a large enough sample of the neighborhood. It's not enough in a neighborhood of five thousand people to make a couple dozen phone calls or drop off twenty fliers. Check out a survey statistics book at the library or check some survey guidelines online. An accurate sample size is necessary if you want to put any faith in your results. The larger the sample size, the more reliable your results.

• If you are utilizing a phone or in-person survey, make sure you get a broad demographic of the neighborhood. In addition to sample size, a good cross sampling of the population will make a difference. For instance, if you make all your phone calls during the day, the majority of people in your sample will be those who don't work outside the home during the day. You'd leave out the input of almost all working folk, which would skew your sample. Again, consult a survey book or website for help.

• Decide if you should conduct your survey by mail, by phone, or in person. Each has advantages, and each has disadvantages. In person or by phone get faster results and require fewer "contacts," but mail is less time intensive and more objective. Bear in mind that most mailed surveys never get returned, which means you have to mail a lot more of them to get a large enough sample for accuracy. Again, consult a book or website for helpful information on the number of mailings you need to prepare and send.

If nothing else, I hope you recognize that a survey is anything but an easy way to listen to the people of your neighborhood. It can be helpful, but must be done carefully. If you decide to use a survey, make sure that you combine it with some other listening approaches.

A Police Ride-Along

Your local police department knows your neighborhood better than almost anyone else. Give them a call and arrange for the members of your team to ride with them on patrol for an evening. Many police departments appreciate the interest and support, and can be very helpful in pointing out aspects of your town that very few people get to see. Of course, for everyone's safety, be sure to comply with all the regulations that are part of this endeavor.

This is another good opportunity to invite more people in your congregation to participate. Who wouldn't love to ride in a police car for a few hours? How exciting that would be! You never know who might step forward to help your team in this aspect of listening.

Meet together at a local coffee shop afterward and share your experiences. How do you see your community differently now than you did before?

A Trip to the Stylist

You know one of the best places to listen to the people of your neighborhood? Seriously, it's the local barbershop or salon. Don't underestimate this amazing listening resource! While you're getting your hair colored or trimmed, do a little bit of eavesdropping (politely, of course). For some reason, people seem to feel quite free to express honest opinions on every matter under the sun when sitting in a chair in front of someone with sharp scissors cutting very near their head. I'm not sure if there's a significant relationship between scissors and expressed opinions, but it does seem to work. Ask a question about any issue in the community, and then sit back and take mental notes. You can do the same thing in the bank, the grocery store, the gas station, a neighborhood pub, and so on.

Next time everyone on your team gets a haircut or manicure or whatever, commit to utilizing this resource. Make a list of questions about which you want to know the answers regarding your neighborhood, and divide them up. Gather in a couple of weeks after everyone has their hair and/or nails done, and share your notes. Again, make sure everyone's listening observations are recorded. Not only will this follow up meeting get you get right down to some significant listening, but it'll probably be the best looking meeting you all attend together!

FOR DISCUSSION:

1. Share a time when someone was attempting to impose their agenda on you (sales, bullies, manipulative acquaintance, religious enthusiast, etc.). How did this event make you feel? How did you respond? Whose agenda won the day?

2. Now share a time when someone genuinely took the time to listen to you and understand your perspective (friend, spouse, counselor, pastor, etc.). How did this event make you feel? How did you respond?

3. Discuss how your church can come off to other people like a sales call during dinner. How does your congregation use those concepts in its everyday goal setting and general expectations? Talk about how that can change.

4. Make sure you also discuss how your congregation genuinely reveals God's love, care, grace, and forgiveness in the neighborhood. Identify ways this is done relationally. Talk about how you can lift these up as desirable ways to reveal God in the community.

5. Make an initial listening plan.

   a. For walking the neighborhood, how will you divide it up? Who will walk when? When will the follow up happen? Who else can you get involved in this?

   b. Is there a local issue around which your neighborhood would gather for a town hall meeting? Who will moderate? Who will speak from each side (if there are two or more sides)? How will publicity be handled? When will your team meet afterward for follow up? Who else can you get involved in this?

   c. If you decide to do a survey, how will you conduct one of the neighborhood? How will you go about setting that up? Will you use a survey service or do it on your own? What information will you seek?

d. Who will call the police or sheriff's department to inquire about a ride-along? How many will participate? Where will you meet afterward? Who else can you get involved in this?

e. For a haircut eavesdropping session, how long will it take for everyone to get their hair done? What questions will you ask? Who will ask them? When will you meet again to follow up? Who else can you get involved in this?

4

Local Demographics—What Is God Doing (and Trying to Do)?

THE PREVIOUS CHAPTER PROVIDED some practical steps to help get you started listening to your neighbors. As important as it is to begin the process of listening to the people of your neighborhood, it's also important to put that listening into some sort of context. Hopefully you, feel some confidence in listening to God and have a plan to begin listening to your neighbors. Continue listening— to God, to your neighbors, and to one another. But as you do so, you need to have a platform on which to begin to place the things you are hearing. A frame of reference—a context—in which God's present day activity can be identified.

The main emphasis of this chapter will therefore be to help you understand and begin the process of seeing a larger picture— what God is already doing in your neighborhood. This involves what some may think of as more worldly than spiritual application, which may seem to some as unfaithful, unchristian, or (dare I say it?) secular. Another whole book should probably be written about the line we attempt to draw in order to separate sacred from secular. This division is almost always less than helpful. That's like saying God is present in some things and some places but not in others. That's kind of silly, don't you think? Isn't Jesus Lord of all creation? Doesn't that include not only devoted Christian people, churches, sacraments, prayer, and ritual, but also business, politics, finances, government, and more? Scripturally, God used a donkey (Num 22), a pagan king (Ezra 1), a worm (Jonah 4), water (Matt 3; Mark 1; Luke 3), mud (John 9), bread and wine (Matt 26; Mark 14; Luke 22), a towel (John 13), an instrument of torture (the cross—see almost every book in the New Testament), and more in order to reveal the presence and reign of God among us. It seems that God can (and does) use whatever God chooses to bring about the reign of God. It's our job to discover how God is at work and join in, not to dictate how we believe God ought to work and limit ourselves to that.

God has always met God's creation in the midst of our current reality. So why can't God use the social sciences, our government, and statistics to reveal the presence and the reign of God among us? Since God is a God of relationship, it only makes sense that God would utilize the things that are part of our lives here and now. After all, God is already present in those things—we may as well point out that presence. Since these are the things of our current day context, it would seem consistent that the God of the Bible would use demographic research, congregational and community records, and a governmental census to show us some ways God is working in our midst today.

Not only can we use contemporary social science information to help give us a context for how God is at work, we can also utilize these things to see what God may be trying to do—where, in fact, God may be inviting our congregations to take a stand, make a difference, speak for God, and be in relationship with God in new kingdom work.

This isn't as tricky or involved as it sounds. It's simply using resources that churches aren't normally accustomed to using. Chances are, however, that some members of your congregation have familiarity with these or similar tools—they just haven't thought to use them for church purposes. Here's another good opportunity to involve some others in your journey. There is an incredible amount of information available through the US Census Bureau, the ARDA, your denomination's website, and even your own congregational records. There's more there than you'll use, but some of this can reveal some pretty cool things about what God is up to in your neighborhood. Some people love digging through this stuff. Grab those people and use them.

DISCOVERING YOUR CONGREGATION

A great place to start is with your own congregation. If you're a newer or a still-in-formation congregation, this could be quick and painless. If you're one of those hundred-year-old-plus places, you'll just get more practice at listening—God's been at work through your congregation for a long time. That's OK. This isn't a race.

Some of your congregational discovery will be your own impressions, some will involve numbers and graphs (yes, I'm talking about the computer—especially Microsoft Excel or Mac Numbers), and some will involve whole groups in your congregation. All are helpful ways to listen to what's going on in your own congregational community. We'll walk through it bit by bit, making sure you have what you need to listen well.

An Overview

The first thing to do is write an overview of your congregation. Include some general information, such as the date your congregation was established, your staff members and roles, key areas of ministry, major projects or pending decisions that are on the table right now. Basically, this is a quick snapshot of your congregation as it is right now. This gets everyone on the same page and helps get you focused. It's amazing how many things we assume everyone knows.

Physical Facilities

Walk around the church property and building(s). Whether you rent or own your space, it is important to take note of the condition and appearance of your facilities. Pay attention to things you may overlook due to familiarity. Why not invite some folks who aren't members of your congregation to come along? Their objectivity can be invaluable.

Property

Similar to the process of walking the neighborhood, look at the landscaping, the sidewalks, the parking lot, the paint or brickwork on the outside of your building, and more. How is the general appearance compared to the rest of your neighborhood? Is your property part of the neighborhood or is it distinct from it? If you were driving by for the first time, would you know where to enter your parking lot? Would you know where to go from there? Would you know how to get into the building? Don't pass judgment, just write this stuff down. Right now you're still listening, gathering information.

Building

Now go inside the building and do a walkthrough. If there's an obvious main entrance, use that. How are the carpets, the lighting, the clutter? If you hadn't been in the building before, would you know where to go to find what you needed (bathrooms, meeting rooms, receptionist, coatrack, or worship)? Wall cracks? Peeling paint? Cobwebs? Is it clean? Are there outdated articles on bulletin boards? Would you get the impression that the people there believe that what happens in this place is important? Is there someone there to greet you and answer your questions? If not, are there times posted and easily seen when someone is there? A phone number? Or perhaps an email and website? How does it smell (this is one area where an objective nose is necessary)? Are there dead insects or rodent droppings? What's the overall mood of the building? Take your time and jot down your impressions. Again, reserve judgment. Just notice.

Building Use

Either before you leave the building or at your next meeting, take the necessary time to consider how the building is used. When you consider your congregation's overall ministries, how does the building help or hinder them? What's working well? Where is flow impeded? Are there ministries that have developed because they work in your building? Are there ministries that have failed (or not been attempted) because of the limitations of your building? Is the building ever over-booked? When does it sit empty? How accessible and safe is the entirety of your building for handicapped, elderly, children? How has your building shaped the style of your ministry?

Church Records

Though not everything can be found in your church records, they will be handy, so make sure they're available. Regardless of the completeness of your records, there are things you can learn, hear, see, and put into perspective. Go dig them out and get ready to do some exploring. Or kindly ask the office manager to gather the information you need. The office manager can very well be your best friend. Make sure that's the case. You don't want to know what life is like if your office manager is ticked at you. Ah, but I digress . . .

As long as you're in the congregational records, you may as well get a couple other things you'll need later. First, from the membership address list, find the three most populous zip codes. In other words, the three zip codes where the highest percentage of your members and affiliates live. Second, break down the membership in a couple of ways: according to age and according to ethnicity. If you want to go further, go ahead and get educational information if you have it: how many have a high school education, some college, 4 year degree, and post-graduate degree. If you've got income information by household, list that too.

Put this information aside, but keep it handy. You'll need it later on.

Membership History

In addition to gathering congregational information, listening to your congregation's records will also involve a computer. Don't freak out if you're not computer savvy. It really isn't that hard for a couple of reasons. First, because once you play around with Microsoft Excel or Mac Numbers, you'll realize that it really can be done. The computer does all the hard parts for you. But second, and more importantly, because this is a great opportunity to involve some other people in your journey. There are people in your congregation who use spreadsheets and charts for their work, or, unbelievably, for fun. Usually, these folks love this stuff and will be glad to help. Plus, you've gained more buy-in and communication to your work. Way to go! Find one or two of these people and get them on board.

Check out the active membership numbers for the history of your congregation. What is the high number and the low number? What years were those? Where are you now in relation to those? Are you trending up or down right now? Do you notice any patterns in the trends? Any thoughts on why that might be? Spend a little bit of time together talking this over. See what insights members of your group may have.

Now do the same for your worship attendance.

Have your computer friends create a line graph showing the membership and worship attendance for each year. If the whole history of your congregation is too long a time, show enough years to capture any trends you've noticed. They can probably pop this out in about ten minutes; but don't actually time them—they likely have something else going on in their lives besides this.

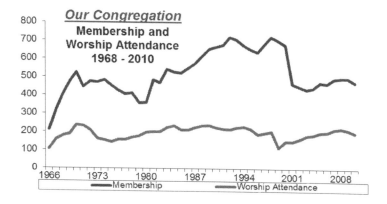

The important thing isn't how big you are, or were, or will be. As countercultural as this is, please don't get caught up in that. The things you're listening for here are the patterns. Are you increasing your numbers for five years, then down for another five? Are you decreasing in worship each year since an all-time high in 1954? Have you increased each year since the congregation began? Don't get too excited about this part—it's just one piece of the congregational puzzle. Make notes of anything your team notices.

Recent Membership Data

Now take a look specifically at the last five years of membership if your congregation is that old. Consider where those years fall within the overall trend of membership. Is anything going on that's different than it was five years ago? Ten years ago?

You're going to add a little more detail to these last five years of membership. If you have this information in your records, list how you received new members for each of those five years. Usually this is in the annual report to the denomination. See? This is why you need to be on good terms with the office manager. Consider these or similar categories: *child baptism* (age 15 and under), *adult baptism* (age 16 and over), *transfer of membership from the same denomination, transfer of membership from a different denomination*, and *affirmation of baptism* (rejoining a church after becoming inactive). What do you notice about how people are joining your congregation? This might give you an idea of who you are listening to (they're more likely to join) and who you're not listening to (they're not).

Now, for the same period of time, list members who have left your congregation. Consider these categories: *death, transfer of membership to the same denomination, transfer of membership to a different denomination,* and *inactivity.* What do you notice about how people are leaving your congregation? Again, this gives you an idea of who feels they aren't being heard (*transfers* and *inactivity*). Note, however, that transfer to a congregation in your area is different than someone who is relocated in their job and transfer to a congregation across the country. Pay attention to these things also.

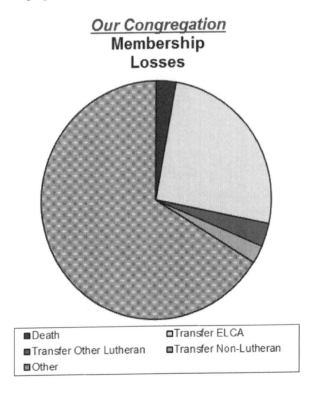

Our Congregation
Membership
Losses

■ Death ☐ Transfer ELCA
■ Transfer Other Lutheran ■ Transfer Non-Lutheran
▨ Other

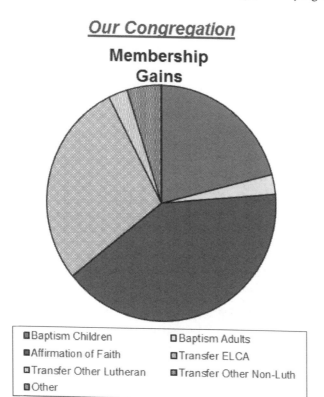

Our Congregation
Membership Gains

- ▣ Baptism Children
- ▣ Affirmation of Faith
- ▢ Transfer Other Lutheran
- ▣ Other
- ▢ Baptism Adults
- ▣ Transfer ELCA
- ▣ Transfer Other Non-Luth

Get your computer friends back again. Ask them to make a couple of pie charts showing categories of people joining and categories of people leaving your congregation. Talk about these percentages for a while. What are you hearing through this information? What are the hopeful signs that are revealed in these numbers? What do they tell you that may be hard to admit?

This isn't about your worth as a congregation, so don't get all arrogant about your "good" numbers and down on yourselves about your "bad" ones. This is much more an indicator about the areas where you are listening relatively well to God and your neighbors, and the areas where you may not be. Every congregation has both, and every congregation always will. Like I said in chapter 2, it's not about avoiding mistakes, it's about acknowledging where we are today and then taking a step forward with God. Then doing it again tomorrow.

Finances

Go back five years in your records and see how many of the following categories you can find for each year. Under the major heading of *Total Income*, separate out the following:

- *Regular giving* (offering),
- *Designated giving* (specific purpose),
- *Grants and partnerships* (denominational support, outside support),
- *Other sources of income* (a trust, interest, investments, sale of property, etc.).

Then categorize for each year your *Total Expenses*, separating out:

- *Operating expenses* (including total personnel),
- *Benevolence* (both budgeted and non-budgeted; include local, denominational, and other),
- *Payments on debts* (including mortgage),
- *Other expenses*.

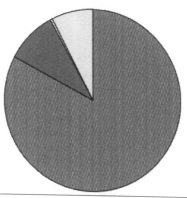

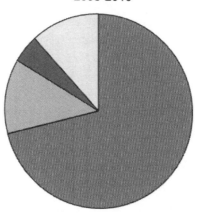

DISCOVERING YOUR NEIGHBORHOOD

Remember in the last chapter all of the listening you did in your neighborhood? And the congregational information on age and ethnicity that you put aside? Gather all that information together. In this section you'll be able to put that into a broader context backed by concrete, social science data. This may not be the most exciting part of this journey of discovery, but it's important. You need to gather as many pieces as you can in order to listen most fully. Next year you won't remember the eye-rolling and the deep sighs as you worked through this section, but you'll return again and again to the information gained here. This is among the most important parts of your listening, so don't take the easy way out now.

This is another good time to recruit some other people for your listening journey. Get some number crunchers, bean counters, financial gurus, or anyone that likes any kind of math. You can recognize some of these by their voices at congregational voting meetings, especially when the annual congregational budget is on the agenda. Sometimes they are the ones that never miss a budget meeting and ask a lot of questions about the budget. Use their gifts in a different way and get them to help with this part of the research. They'll appreciate being asked.

All the information that is gathered every ten years in by the US Census Bureau is readily available for stuff just like this. Someone else has already done the listening; all you have to do is pick up the information.

Your denomination may have great demographic information on its website. Be sure to check there, as it may be easier to get information you need through them. They may have all you need right there. But if not, or if you want more, the US Census Bureau has done an amazing amount of work for you. Here's how to find the information they have for you.

Go to the U.S. Census Bureau website www.census.gov. At the very bottom of the page, click on the "American FactFinder" link in the "Find Data" column. Once American FactFinder opens, type in the zip code, town, or county in which you are interested.

Click "Go." A smaller window will open with population information and further links for more specific information, e.g., "Race and Hispanic or Latino Origin" or "Households and Families." Click on the link called "General Population and Housing Characteristics." You'll see a chart with information on ages, male and female, race, and more. You can go back and find any information that you think may be relevant.

Do this for all three primary zip codes that make up your congregation's neighborhood. You discovered these when you were looking at your congregational records previously in this chapter. Once you have the population information on your three zip codes, go back to the main American FactFinder page to begin looking at the sets of information you want to gather.

You'll want to be able to use this information, so be sure to write it down or chart it out. Here are some things you'll want to include in your searching. Be sure to check all three of the zip codes you've identified as comprising your neighborhood.

- Overall population of primary zip code(s), town, county
- Age distribution in primary zip code(s), town, county
- Educational Level of primary zip code(s), town, county
- Financial income in primary zip code(s), town, county
- Percentage of households (especially note children below 18 years of age) living below the poverty line in primary zip code(s), town, county
- Ethnic makeup of primary zip code(s), town, county
- Primary language of primary zip code(s), town, county

Your town or county website may have information available on traffic flow and patterns. Discovering how many cars per day go by your church property can be really helpful in deciding how to strengthen relationships with people who drive through your neighborhood on their way to work.

Another website to check is www.thearda.com, or *The Association of Religious Data Archives*. This is a very easy-to-navigate website and can give great information about church populations in your county and state. You can find actual population for your denomination or association, worship attendance numbers, trends, and lots of other fun and interesting stuff. Be sure to spend sufficient time on the ARDA website.

Put all the gathered information in chart form, utilizing the talents of your computer savvy people. Gather your team together over dinner and spend an evening looking it over. As you gather with all this information, what trends do you see? Check for helpful information about your primary zip codes (neighborhood), town, and county. For example, is the major ethnic group increasing in percentage in your area, decreasing, or remaining the same? How does that compare to your city and county? How well educated is your area compared to the rest of the county? Does your congregation have close to the same median age as your neighborhood? If not, why not? Is there a higher percentage of people involved in churches or lower over time? Which denominations or congregations are people joining? Which denominations or congregations are declining? Why might that be? Based on this research, what might your community look like ten years from now? What surprises have you discovered about your neighborhood, town, or county?

Compare these findings with your other neighborhood listening activities. How do all these pieces fit together? Does all the information reveal the same things or are there apparent discrepancies? How can any discrepancies be explained, or can they?

Take your time and have fun talking through all this information. See what new discoveries you can make about your neighborhood. All this listening is making you an expert on your neighborhood.

After you feel like you've digested the information about your neighborhood, write down the things that seem important to you. This could be themes that continue to emerge, trends of which you weren't aware, or information that caught you by surprise. This serves as a summary of your listening and will be invaluable in the months and years to come.

Now try seeing how your congregation fits into it. Compare your congregational makeup to the surrounding neighborhood. How closely does your congregation resemble the broader community? If there are large differences between the neighborhood and your congregation (e.g., a congregation older than the neighborhood, more educated, more white, etc.), that might help reveal who is being listened to by your congregation. That can be helpful in planning relationship strategies later on.

When you feel you've worked with this information together long enough to be fairly comfortable with it, put it aside temporarily. Don't make too many plans around it yet. There are still a couple of things to do before you get too specific about congregational direction and concrete planning.

FOR DISCUSSION:

As you look back over all these charts and data, is there anything surprising to you in the information gathered? Anything you didn't know before?

1. What would you say is the most important thing you discovered about your congregation? About your neighborhood?

2. In what demographic area is your congregation closest your neighborhood, e.g., education, ethnicity, median age?

3. In what demographic area is your congregation least like your neighborhood? Why do you suppose that is?

5

We're All in This Together— Relationships Already Exist

A TRADITIONAL YIDDISH SAYING goes like this, "Sure a bird could marry a fish, but where would they live?"[1] This is the dilemma many congregations believe they face. Some congregations think of themselves as so different from their surrounding neighborhoods that they have a difficult time figuring out how to relate to that broader community, or even if they should. These congregational communities say that they are spiritual communities, and the neighborhoods around them are secular. They say they are communities created to honor God, and the world around them has no desire to do so, therefore a relationship isn't possible without the conversion of the neighborhood occurring first. They may even say that they have about as much in common with their immediate neighborhoods as a bird has with a fish.

While it is true that congregations are created by God through the Holy Spirit in the name of Jesus, each congregation is created and placed by this same God as part of a neighborhood. These congregational communities are called to be present within

---

1. Schwartz, "Forming a New Congregation," 1.

their surrounding neighborhood and in relationship with them. According to Scott Frederickson, congregations that struggle with their role in the neighborhood often attempt to solve their perceived *bird and fish* quandary by *over contextualization*, i.e., blurring their historic values in order to relate to their surrounding communities, or by *under contextualization*, isolating themselves from their environment to remain a holy refuge for those who seek it.[2] These two extremes involve the thinking that either the bird attempts to become a fish, or the bird cannot relate to the fish at all. The reality is, however, that the bird and fish analogy is based on a false assumption, as congregations already do relate to their neighborhoods; just sometimes not on purpose.

Although congregations may really differ from their surrounding neighborhoods, they are yet made up of people who live and breathe within that neighborhood. People who make up local congregations are also people who've been shaped by, and who shape, the values, identities, and cultures of their neighborhoods. It must be remembered that church members are also community members; the bird and the fish analogy simply doesn't apply at all. Churches and their contexts are already in relationship, and in order for churches to live missionally as they are created to be, they need first to recognize this relationship that already exists within their environment.

Growing up as a Roman Catholic in Ogden, Utah, the differences between my congregation and my surrounding culture were obvious and striking. Words such as "Primary," "Mutual," "Relief Society," "Ward," "Stake," and "Word of Wisdom," that were commonly understood in my neighborhood and at the public school were not a part of the vocabulary of my church environment. The reverse was also true. Language in my parish, including phrases such as "Holy Day of Obligation," "Immaculate Conception," "Stations of the Cross," "Patron Saint," and "Eucharist" were almost entirely unknown in my non-Catholic neighborhood. I lived in two worlds, and there was little, if any, attempt by either to interrelate with the other. There was virtually no deliberate relationship

2. Frederickson, *Missional Church in Context*, 44.

between my home parish and my home neighborhood, with the result that my congregation had no real desire to be in a mutual relationship with the neighborhood. True, my congregation would have preferred that the entire neighborhood become Roman Catholic, but everyone was pretty sure this was not going to happen. Once in a while, one of the non-Catholics in the neighborhood would convert, and there was celebration over this apparent victory, especially if the new convert had been Mormon. But just as often, there was loss, as members left Catholicism and joined the LDS Church (Church of Jesus Christ of Latter Day Saints).

For me, church was a secluded, private society that had its own agenda and its own path. Conveniently located a mile from my house, my parish congregation was an organization that gave guidance to its members in order to help them operate within the church culture. It attempted to exist virtually unto itself in the context of the surrounding LDS culture. The understood dichotomy of these two cultures of my world was difficult in and of itself, and the expectations imposed by each culture made it more difficult yet.

I grew up wondering what, if any, was the relationship between these two cultures that co-existed within my neighborhood. My assumption was that if either culture was influenced by the other in any significant way, it would compromise its identity, its values, and its position in the world. Each thought it had to be maintained independently of the other in order for it to be what it was designed to be. Neither seemed to understand that they actually were part of the same neighborhood and shared many neighborhood values and concepts. The relationship between my parish congregation and my LDS neighborhood already existed, it's just that neither wanted to admit it or enter more deliberately into it. Neither wanted to seek the presence of God that already exists within those relationships and lift it up, point it out, and participate with God in mercy, love, and forgiveness there.

Congregations are not to live in isolation, but in mutual relationship in and with their context. This is essential to their missional identity. The perichoretic nature of the triune God is the perfect relationship, and is the source of the church's relationship with the world. As the triune God engages in relationship with the world, this God is also therefore engaging in a relationship with the church as part of the world. Each congregation is created, called, and sent to live out this missional relationship with God, with its own members (and the rest of the church), and with the world.

It's not that we as congregations have to start at square one and work at developing some kind of relationship with our neighborhoods. Lots of relationships already exist. Our kids go to the same schools, most of us are connected through the same power grid, we buy food at the same grocery stores, we use the same cell towers, we watch the same TV shows, we use the same currency, and so on. It's not so much that the church is separated from the neighborhood; it's that we don't consider these relationships to be important. God is already at work in the neighborhood, and through the relationships we have; we can point that out and participate with God in that work. Relationships are the nature of God, remember?

FOR DISCUSSION:

1. How many relationships between your congregation and your neighborhood can you identify?

2. What agencies or institutions in the neighborhood/community does your *congregation* support, either with finances, volunteers, staff, or in an advisory capacity?

3. What agencies or institutions in the neighborhood/community do *individual members* of your congregation support, either with finances, as volunteers, as staff members, or by serving on a board of directors?

4. Where is God at work in those agencies, even if they aren't Christian in their orientation or understanding?

5. How can those relationships be lifted up as holy relationships with the work of those agencies being recognized in your congregation as holy work?

6

Modeling Vulnerability
in Relationship

Do you remember the first time you told someone that you loved them, other than your mom? Do you remember the moments leading up to your heartfelt declaration of adoration: the nervousness, the butterflies in your stomach, the almost sick feeling of being so far out on a limb—so exposed? What if she doesn't love me in return? What if he laughs? How will I deal with the devastation if I'm making a huge mistake here?

There's nothing as frightening as vulnerability—that feeling of helplessness, of knowing your life is entirely in the hands of someone else. That vulnerable moment when you express your love could lead to the other person humiliating you. Or it could be the point at which your relationship deepens, defines your life direction, and becomes—I have to throw this in—perichoretic. Vulnerability is necessary for trust. And trust is necessary to have a relationship. And relationship is the nature of God.

You could say that God is God because God is vulnerable. That's not one of the adjectives we usually use to describe God, but isn't it true? In the Garden of Gethsemane, Jesus indicated he had the option to call down twelve legions of angels (Matt 26:53) to fight for him with heavenly power and might. But that wasn't what his role was. That wasn't who *he* was. Like a lamb led to the slaughter (Isa 53:7 and Acts 8:32), Jesus became the epitome of vulnerability. It was risky. It was necessary. It was Godly. It revealed the nature of a relational God who takes risks of vulnerability for the sake of developing a loving relationship with the world. With us. After listening, vulnerability is the next step in developing relationship—in revealing the reign of God in the world.

Up until now you've been doing a lot of listening. Well and good, necessary, and the first part of relationship. But let's face it, because it can be done kind of clinically, listening can also be pretty safe. It's one thing to listen and another to be vulnerable.

Do you recall the *Dancing with the Stars* analogy back in chapter 1? The reason those couples are able to do those amazing dance routines is that they have developed trust for each other. One person knows what the other is supposed to do and trusts them to do it—otherwise there could be serious injury, or at least serious embarrassment. When one partner jumps, she trusts the other partner to catch her. When one partner leans backward, he trusts the other partner to counter balance with her own weight. We could analyze the physics involved, or simply recognize that when each partner knows and trusts what the other will do, each is then free to do her/his own part of the routine without concern.

That trust is not automatic, though. It takes time, practice, and the experience of lots of mistakes to form. The first time a step is tried, it probably won't work correctly, and both dance partners are likely to experience some falls. This is part of the process of learning a routine, of developing trust in one another. Stumbles are merely a part of developing a relationship.

Knowing they will make mistakes, knowing they will risk injury, the dancers are willing to try anyway. It's like each is willing early on to say, "If this is going to work, I'm going to have to trust you. I don't yet know if you are trustworthy, but I'm going to attempt to trust you anyway. Let's see what happens." Being willing to trust when there's a risk of failing makes one feel quite vulnerable. It's not easy, not fun, and not safe. And yet vulnerability is a necessary part of trust-building, a key aspect of relationships. Being willing to risk these ungraceful spills involves vulnerability. And that's where we're going now.

During this process, you've probably begun to form some trust among yourselves as a team. You've been praying together (right?), studying Scripture together, discussing the strengths and weaknesses of the congregation about which you care deeply, listening to your neighborhood, and spending time together. Awesome! Let's get a little more intentional about it. At the end of this chapter you'll be stepping into vulnerability. Feel the excitement?

Other than the explanations in the first part of this chapter, there's a reason for doing this. You'll be asking your congregation to take a step toward living more fully as a community that bears the name of Christ. They will be growing in their ability to reveal the nature of God among themselves, and therefore to the world. That's what the church is here for, after all.

Now, you can just tell them to do that. You can try to describe it for them and then strongly suggest they try it themselves. You can even wax poetic about the beautiful and godly attributes of a faith community that lives together in love and trust.

Yeah, good luck with that. There are already too many churches that tell people what they ought to be doing. No, you have a much more significant tool to utilize. You can model it. You can be the leaven in the dough. You can live relationally—perichoretically—in the midst of your congregation and reveal what God is doing among you. You can be vulnerable. Without guarantees. Without promises. Without demanded outcomes. Just being in relationship as modeled by the vulnerable, relational, perichoretic, triune God. Go with God working in you and in your congregation.

Follow the discussion questions at the end of this chapter. See what happens and spend some time talking about how you feel. Then take this chapter and these discussion questions to other groups in your congregation. Try them out with your council, small groups, choir, Bible studies, quilters, snow shovelers, lawn mowers, whatever. Explain that this is a part of your "Listening to God" task force and that you're required to do it with them; the mean author of this book is making you do it. This may get you in the door, but probably won't ease your sense of vulnerability. Make sure you spend follow-up time with them to help them put this experience into context—that this is a *perichoretic* experience. Yup, teach them this word, that it reveals the nature of God, and helps us enter into deeper relationships with one another. It is the beginning of how we are to enter into relationships with our neighbors. Plus, if you can explain the meaning of words like *perichoretic*, they'll be much more inclined to think you know what you're talking about.

We don't claim power and authority over our neighborhood; we claim relationality in the name of Jesus. We listen carefully to our neighbors, acknowledge our own imperfections and struggles, and experience God's redemption and care together. We partner with them in ways that help us participate with God in God's mission. But I'm getting ahead of myself. All that comes in the next chapter.

FOR DISCUSSION:

1. Make sure you are all sitting in a circle without a table in center. Discuss together any impressions you have about this chapter or about this book so far. What's helpful? What's challenging? What's less than helpful? What have you learned?

2. Make a confidentiality covenant within your group. Whatever is shared in the group stays in the group. Assure one another that this is a safe place, a place where all can be vulnerable.

3. Everyone walks around every day carrying baggage. Fears, difficulties, anxieties, stresses, hopes, dreams. We often keep these to ourselves for fear of being too vulnerable. Think about the most important thing that's going on in your life right now. It can be something causing you anxiety or something causing you excitement. To begin practicing trust, share this important part of your life with the gathered group. Allow as much time as necessary for all to take part.

4. As this is going on, pay special attention to the person on your left when they share. Remember what they are telling the group and why this part of their lives is so important.

5. After all have shared, go back around the circle and pray for one another. Have each person in the group pray for the person on their left (that's why you listened so carefully to them!). Again, allow as much time as necessary for this process. When all have prayed, join hands and pray the Lord's Prayer together.

6. Try this out with other groups, teams, committees in your congregation. Listen to the feedback that comes both immediately and later on.

7

Putting It All Together— Joining God's Activity in Your Neighborhood

IT'S TIME TO TAKE all this material, all this information, all this experience, and put it together in a way that can be understood as well as be helpful. You need to do this for a couple of reasons. First, as a review to make certain you know what you've been doing for all this time; second, so that you can present it to your leadership board and to the congregation for their input. Only when they have a grasp of what you've come to understand will they be able to participate in it. And their input and buy-in is vital—communication and transparency, after all. They will come up with things you haven't seen and clarify some things you didn't know needed clarifying. Awesome! We do this together, not independently. The final say on the specifics of your congregational participation with God in the neighborhood is theirs. Your job has been to help them be able to do that from a perspective that reflects what God is already about in your neighborhood.

PUTTING THIS ALL TOGETHER

Take the charts and graphs that you've made up to this point and put them into one document on a computer. Be sure to include a brief synopsis of your notes and observations related to each part. This will likely be several pages, but that's OK. Don't worry about making this presentable, as you won't be presenting it. This is primarily for your team so you can review, clarify, and plan what you will be presenting.

Spend some time reviewing and sharing your information together. Talk about trends and changes in your congregation and in the neighborhood. Note how God has been present with you. Share together how you've grown in your ability to listen to God, each other, and the neighborhood. Discuss how much better you are able to understand, to relate, to participate with God in God's mission. Seek to be specific and clear.

PARTICIPATE IN A SWOC ANALYSIS

You probably know your congregation and neighborhood better than anyone at this point. You are in a great place to begin a preliminary analysis of God's direction. One very helpful way to begin is with a SWOC analysis. SWOC is an acronym for Strengths, Weaknesses, Opportunities, and Challenges. This can be quite revealing and is a solid way to distill down to reasonable pieces all the information and knowledge you have gained.

Begin by placing four sheets of paper on a table or attach them to a wall. Title the first one "Strengths," the next one "Weaknesses," another "Opportunities," and the last "Challenges." Have the members of your group write what they see as appropriate words or phrases on each. There's no right or wrong, necessarily. Knowing what you know, what are your congregational strengths? That might include such things as "visionary leadership," "our building," "spiritual depth," or "good reputation in the neighborhood." Be honest and realistic. These are the gifts that God has given to you. Claim them!

Make sure you are honest about your weaknesses too. Such things as "unkempt facility," "lack of parking," "poor finances," or "difficulty with changes" don't make you a lesser congregation; but they are areas where you aren't likely to excel at this point in time. It may mean simply that God isn't calling you to develop relationships in your neighborhood based on these characteristics. Don't worry about them, but you do need to be aware of them.

Consider the opportunities that are available in your neighborhood. New housing developments, new immigrant families, active food pantry or homeless shelter needing support, empty buildings looking for renters and more may fit this category. You've done all the research, you know what the opportunities are. Take sufficient time here, as this is an area where congregations don't always have a lot of practice.

What challenges have to be overcome in order to take advantage of these opportunities? If you neighborhood is experiencing transition to a minority population (an opportunity), is a prevailing cultural racism making relationships hard? Does a congregational attitude of fear inhibit branching into new ministry areas?

WHAT IS GOD DOING?

Now move to the next exercise. With what you know about God and God's activity through biblical history, list on another sheet of paper how you see God at work in your congregation and in your neighborhood. What is happening anywhere, through anyone, that is consistent with God's mission?

Any surprises? What can you learn about God from the work God is doing in your neighborhood? How do the strengths of your congregation allow you to join more fully in support of this activity? In what areas are you weak as a congregation, where God may not be calling you to participate, but where you can proclaim and point out God's activity?

WHAT IS GOD TRYING TO DO?

Let's go beyond the here and now. In keeping with your understanding of God and God's intention in the world, what might God be trying to do or getting ready to do? Write these down on a separate sheet. Then step back, look at all of the writing on these sheets, and look at possible overlaps or connections.

What opportunities may be presenting themselves in the near future? What trends may be arising that could open some doors for your congregation to join with God? Where is the presence of God not being revealed or not being seen, and could your congregation step in with God's relational love and mercy? As you consider your congregational strengths, what opportunities might God be inviting you to initiate? With whom can you partner? Are there any agencies or institutions already working in these areas that need your help? What can you offer? How can you develop a relationship where those individuals/agencies can help you too?

GOVERNING BOARD INPUT

Prepare a presentation for your leadership or governing board. Decide who will present each chart and how long you'll spend presenting it. Less may be more here! You need to remember that you've been deeply involved in this process for quite a while; they aren't as steeped in it yet. Give them an overview of important facts and trends in a few minutes. Be sure to practice the whole presentation, making sure to time it. Depending on your congregation's standard board meeting, it's probably best to keep this part of the presentation to less than half an hour. Be sure to allow time for questions afterward.

After presenting your basic findings, follow the same pattern you did together as a group. Lead your governing board through their own SWOC analysis. Don't bias them with your group's SWOC results; let them do this on their own.

Then lead them through a "What Is God Doing?" and a "What Is God Trying to Do?" exercise. Again, allow them to draw their own conclusions and discover this for themselves.

After all this is done, spend some time considering the direction God seems to be moving and how your congregation has been equipped to participate. Brainstorm on this for a while, allowing any ideas to flow. Be sure to have someone writing them down on a large sheet posted on the wall. Ask your leaders to be as specific as possible at this point. We're well past the theory phase and deeply into the realities of God's work right here and right now.

Once the brainstorming has slowed down, take some time to pray—either silently or aloud. Ask God to move among you and God's Spirit to inspire you to recognize God's purpose for your congregation.

Then hand out five sticky dots to each council member. Have them place their dots on any of the specific brainstormed ideas they think God is truly calling them to step into. They can place all five dots on one idea or distribute them in any way they believe appropriate.

After all have placed their dots, see which ideas are coming forth as priorities as seen by your leadership group. These ideas, obviously, will be the ones with the most dots attached. The office manager of the leadership board should then write these prioritized ideas down. Send the council home to pray and discern what God has just done among them.

CONGREGATIONAL INPUT

Before your governing board gets too carried away with making plans, make sure to allow time for the congregation as a whole to have input in the congregation's direction. Set up a congregational meeting by whatever means are appropriate in your tradition, and follow the same process as you did with your leaders. Present your findings, do a SWOC analysis, and allow input on "What Is God Doing?" and "What Is God Trying to Do?" Brainstorm, pray, and prioritize. As a practical thought, depending on the size of your congregation, when you get to the sticky dots, you may want to limit the number given to each person to two or three.

This can be very exciting and uplifting for your congregation. They can see some practical, real-life ways that God is calling them into their neighborhood. They can put flesh and blood on their faith. They can see some ways that being a disciple of Jesus actually does have an effect on the world. Their Christianity takes on a new life as they follow the Holy Spirit into the broader community. And, your congregation begins to see its purpose from the perspective of God's mission rather than their own survival and benefit.

Make sure that your governing board has all the input from you and from the congregation. They are now equipped to help the congregation catch the wind of the Spirit and join God's activity in the world, and specifically in your neighborhood. They can now develop some clear plans and timetables for your congregation to act—confident that you are all in keeping with God's activity and God's mission. Plus, they already have congregational buy-in.

Perhaps your governing board will ask you to come up with the clear plan of action for the congregation. That would be great! It is a separate agenda, quite different from what your group has been doing so far. Therefore you should allow each member the opportunity to sign up for that step—allowing them to choose not to participate if they feel they aren't called to do the planning part. Either way, your congregation can confidently proclaim, point out, and participate in the reign of God present in your neighborhood. Within your neighborhood you are bearing the fruit of the kingdom of God, and that's what the church is here for, after all.

Make sure you let me know how this goes for you. I'd love to celebrate your insights, your direction, and your relational ministry!

The Lord is with you. God has placed your congregation in your surrounding community on purpose. You are being called by the Holy Spirit to be part of Christ's redeeming work in that neighborhood. Hallelujah! It's good to be the church, isn't it?

Appendix A

Foundation for Mission Bible Study

SESSION 1

Genesis 1:29—2:1

> God said, "See, I have given you every plant yielding seed that is upon the face of all the earth, and every tree with seed in its fruit; you shall have them for food. *[30]* And to every beast of the earth, and to every bird of the air, and to everything that creeps on the earth, everything that has the breath of life, I have given every green plant for food." And it was so. *[31]* God saw everything that he had made, and indeed, it was very good. And there was evening and there was morning, the sixth day. *[2:1]* Thus the heavens and the earth were finished, and all their multitude.

- What does this text say about who God is and what God is like?
- What does it say about God's relationship with the Hebrew people who, in the face of cultural pressure, loudly proclaim ONE God who is and does these things?
- What signs of this God can we see?

SESSION 2

Genesis 2:7–9

> Then the LORD God formed man from the dust of the ground, and breathed into his nostrils the breath of life; and the man became a living being. *[8]* And the LORD God planted a garden in Eden, in the east; and there he put the man whom he had formed. *[9]* Out of the ground the LORD God made to grow every tree that is pleasant to the sight and good for food, the tree of life also in the midst of the garden, and the tree of the knowledge of good and evil.

- What does this text say about who God is and what God is like?
- What does it say about God's relationship with the Hebrew people who, in the face of cultural pressure, loudly proclaim one God who is and does these things?
- What signs of this God can we see?

SESSION 3

Genesis 3:1–7, 21

> Now the serpent was more crafty than any other wild animal that the LORD God had made. He said to the woman, "Did God say, 'You shall not eat from any tree in the garden'?" *[2]* The woman said to the serpent, "We may eat of the fruit of the trees in the garden; *[3]* but God said, 'You shall not eat of the fruit of the tree that is in the middle of the garden, nor shall you touch it, or you shall die.'" *[4]* But the serpent said to the woman, "You will not die; *[5]* for God knows that when you eat of it your eyes will be opened, and you will be like God, knowing good and evil." *[6]* So when the woman saw that the tree was good for food, and that it was a delight to the eyes, and that the tree was to be desired to make one wise, she took of its fruit and ate; and she also gave some

to her husband, who was with her, and he ate. *[7]* Then the eyes of both were opened, and they knew that they were naked; and they sewed fig leaves together and made loincloths for themselves. . . . *[3:21]* And the LORD God made garments of skins for the man and for his wife, and clothed them.

- What was so wrong with the eating of this fruit "to make one wise"?

- Why did Adam and Eve find it necessary to cover themselves, once their eyes "were opened"?

- Especially considering the culture and the times, what is so unusual about God's response to this betrayal in verse 21?

- What does that say about God's attitude toward today's sinful world?

SESSION 4

Genesis 9:8–13

Then God said to Noah and to his sons with him, *[9]* "As for me, I am establishing my covenant with you and your descendants after you, *[10]* and with every living creature that is with you, the birds, the domestic animals, and every animal of the earth with you, as many as came out of the ark. *[11]* I establish my covenant with you, that never again shall all flesh be cut off by the waters of a flood, and never again shall there be a flood to destroy the earth." *[12]* God said, "This is the sign of the covenant that I make between me and you and every living creature that is with you, for all future generations: *[13]* I have set my bow in the clouds, and it shall be a sign of the covenant between me and the earth."

- What was the covenant between God and every living creature for all future generations?

- Remembering that God flooded the world to rid it of all evil and wickedness, what characteristics of God does this story reveal?

- How are these attributes of God being revealed in our world today?

SESSION 5

Genesis 12:1–3

> Now the LORD said to Abram, "Go from your country and your kindred and your father's house to the land that I will show you. *[2]* I will make of you a great nation, and I will bless you, and make your name great, so that you will be a blessing. *[3]* I will bless those who bless you, and the one who curses you I will curse; and in you all the families of the earth shall be blessed."

- What was God's intention with Abram (Abraham)?

- Can you think of a more certain way for God to have accomplished this?

- Why does God take this risk?

SESSION 6

Exodus 20:1–17

> Then God spoke all these words: *[2]* I am the LORD your God, who brought you out of the land of Egypt, out of the house of slavery; *[3]* you shall have no other gods before me. *[4]* You shall not make for yourself an idol, whether in the form of anything that is in heaven above, or that is on the earth beneath, or that is in the water under the earth. *[5]* You shall not bow down to them or worship them; for I the LORD your God am a jealous God, punishing children for the iniquity of parents, to the third

and the fourth generation of those who reject me, *[6]* but showing steadfast love to the thousandth generation of those who love me and keep my commandments. *[7]* You shall not make wrongful use of the name of the LORD your God, for the LORD will not acquit anyone who misuses his name. *[8]* Remember the sabbath day, and keep it holy. *[9]* Six days you shall labor and do all your work. *[10]* But the seventh day is a sabbath to the LORD your God; you shall not do any work—you, your son or your daughter, your male or female slave, your livestock, or the alien resident in your towns. *[11]* For in six days the LORD made heaven and earth, the sea, and all that is in them, but rested the seventh day; therefore the LORD blessed the sabbath day and consecrated it. *[12]* Honor your father and your mother, so that your days may be long in the land that the LORD your God is giving you. *[13]* You shall not murder. *[14]* You shall not commit adultery. *[15]* You shall not steal. *[16]* You shall not bear false witness against your neighbor. *[17]* You shall not covet your neighbor's house; you shall not covet your neighbor's wife, or male or female slave, or ox, or donkey, or anything that belongs to your neighbor.

- Considering what these texts so far have revealed about God and God's intentions, what new insights does that give you around why God gave the 10 Commandments?

SESSION 7

Jeremiah 31:31–34

The days are surely coming, says the LORD, when I will make a new covenant with the house of Israel and the house of Judah. *[32]* It will not be like the covenant that I made with their ancestors when I took them by the hand to bring them out of the land of Egypt—a covenant that they broke, though I was their husband, says the LORD. *[33]* But this is the covenant that I will make with the house of Israel after those days, says the LORD: I will put my law within them, and I will write it on their hearts; and I will be their God, and they shall be my people. [34] No longer shall they teach one another, or say to each other, "Know the LORD," for they shall all know me, from the least of them to the greatest, says the LORD; for I will forgive their iniquity, and remember their sin no more.

- How is this covenant different than the previous ones?

- If this covenant is so much better, why didn't God establish this one in the first place?

- Is God changing God's mind, or is something else going on?

SESSION 8

Matthew 26:26–29

While they were eating, Jesus took a loaf of bread, and after blessing it he broke it, gave it to the disciples, and said, "Take, eat; this is my body." [27] Then he took a cup, and after giving thanks he gave it to them, saying, "Drink from it, all of you; [28] for this is my blood of the covenant, which is poured out for many for the forgiveness of sins. [29] I tell you, I will never again drink of this fruit of the vine until that day when I drink it new with you in my Father's kingdom."

- Another covenant. How is this one different?

- Why does God need still another covenant?

- How does this one fit with what we know and have discovered so far about God and God's missional activity in the world?

SESSION 9

Acts 2:1–4

> When the day of Pentecost had come, they were all to-
> gether in one place. *[2]* And suddenly from heaven there
> came a sound like the rush of a violent wind, and it filled
> the entire house where they were sitting. *[3]* Divided
> tongues, as of fire, appeared among them, and a tongue
> rested on each of them. *[4]* All of them were filled with
> the Holy Spirit and began to speak in other languages, as
> the Spirit gave them ability.

- Apparently, God isn't done yet. The covenant of Jesus'
  body and blood on the cross doesn't end God's work. What
  is God doing?
- This isn't just the twelve apostles; it is *all* the disciples. What
  does that say about the role of the church today?
- Lutherans proclaim the "priesthood of all believers" as a core
  doctrine. How do you see that fitting in with the church today?

SESSION 10

Acts 2:37–39

> Now when they heard this, they were cut to the heart and
> said to Peter and to the other apostles, "Brothers, what
> should we do?" *[38]* Peter said to them, "Repent, and be
> baptized every one of you in the name of Jesus Christ so
> that your sins may be forgiven; and you will receive the
> gift of the Holy Spirit. *[39]* For the promise is for you,
> for your children, and for all who are far away, everyone
> whom the Lord our God calls to him."

- How do you see Peter's speech in light of God's action in
  creation so far?
- Where does this fit in the overall scheme of God's mission?

- What insights do you gain about the job of the church today?

- What missional difference does it make to see God's intentions starting in Genesis, as opposed to starting with the cross?

Bibliography

Bosch, David Jacobus. *Transforming Mission: Paradigm Shifts in Theology of Mission*. American Society of Missiology 16. Maryknoll: Orbis, 1991.

Frederickson, Scott. *The Missional Church in Context: Helping Congregations Develop Contextual Ministry*. Edited by Craig Van Gelder. Grand Rapids: Eerdmans, 2007.

Fryer, Kelly A. *Reclaiming the "L" Word: Renewing the Church from Its Lutheran Core*. Minneapolis: Augsburg, 2003.

Gittins, Anthony J. *Ministry at the Margins: Strategy and Spirituality for Mission*. Maryknoll: Orbis, 2002.

Luther, Martin. *Letters 1*. Vol. 48 of *Luther's Works*. Edited and translated by Gottfried G. Krodel. Philadelphia: Fortress, 1963.

Moltmann, Jürgen. "Perichoresis: An Old Magic Word for a New Trinitarian Theology." In *Trinity, Community, and Power: Mapping Trajectories in Wesleyan Theology*, edited by M. Douglas Meeks, 113–14. Nashville: Kingswood, 2000.

Newbigin, Lesslie. *The Gospel in a Pluralist Society*. Grand Rapids: Eerdmans, 1989.

Schwartz, Barry. "Forming a New Congregation: The Uneasy Tension between Freedom and Community." *Reconstructionist* 60 (1995) 1.

Sharratt, Michael. *Galileo: Decisive Innovator*. Oxford: Blackwell, 1994.

Van Gelder, Craig. *The Missional Church in Context: Helping Congregations Develop Contextual Ministry*. Grand Rapids: Eerdmans, 2007.

76222277R00055

Made in the USA
Lexington, KY
22 December 2017